AS IF SEEN
AT AN ANGLE

As If Seen at an Angle

Kevin O'Rourke

TINDERBOX
EDITIONS

Tinderbox Editions
Molly Sutton Kiefer, Publisher and Editor
Red Wing, Minnesota
tinderboxeditions@gmail.com
www.tinderboxeditions.org

Cover design by Nikkita Cohoon
Cover art by Jennie Ottinger, "Operating," oil on canvas, 2012
Interior design by Nikkita Cohoon
Author photo by Ellen Hurst

All we are is representation, what we appear to be & are, & are not
And representation is all we remember.

Something hesitating & looking back & caught for a moment

—Larry Levis

The years will scab over,
            impossible not to pick at them.

—Forrest Gander

CONTENTS

IV

AS IF SEEN
AT AN ANGLE

On Inquiry

One could begin by simply looking. Then by describing what one sees, what color it is, how big, how dark, how often, its tones and gradations, and so then discovering other things to describe, things that, by being described, help one better understand the inquiry's source. For what do we do when we look—when we *really* look, when we crane our necks for a better view—but discover the details of the thing being looked at? Maybe we can't sculpt, maybe our paint has gone dry in its tubes, our pencils dull and sketchbooks mislaid in boxes of forget-me-nots, but by looking we can all be artists of some sort, rendering if only for ourselves the truth of the world as we see it. After all, "art," said the painter Gerhard Richter, "is the highest form of hope."

But hope in what? One could look at a leaf all day—doing so will not necessarily lead to a understanding of that leaf. Maybe, then, study is wanted, study so rigorous that it has its own vocabulary and is an occluded mystery to the uninitiated. All the amateurs see are the experts' shadows, and the billowing white of their lab coats as they sweep down hallways stark with fluorescence to confirm that yes, eventually, the worst of our fears will be confirmed and yes, we are in their power. Trust us, they say, for we know the mysteries of cell and bacterium, the malevolent demigods with which we are constantly intimate and which our children sneeze onto our hands. Maybe, then, the highest form of hope is that we will understand our fate when it befalls us by having come to some understanding of the world beforehand via observation and description.

But to describe our world we need words, which themselves invite inquiries of their own, hence the nested doll that is etymology, the root of which comes from the Ancient Greek *etymologia*, "study of the true sense (of a word)." Which is tricky, the definition containing the old chestnut *true*, a word that by simply existing divides the world into light and dark, yes and no, and creates the gulfs between those far shores of disagreement. Words, then, are an imprecise tool at best, as apt to cause injury as cure. And words will inevitably fail us, as our bodies and all the bodies of those we love will inevitably fail. Our world is one of inevitably irrevocably failing bodies trying to make some sense of our failures, our bodies creaking aging wooden windmills barely hanging on to the soil in a rain-stricken landscape. Words, said the writer James Agee, "cannot embody; they can only describe. But a certain kind of artist … despises this fact about words or his medium, and continually brings words as near as he can to an illusion of embodiment."

But embodiments—the giving of tangible form or spirit to that which is intangible—even the illusions thereof, do not happen by themselves. They need beginnings, and the toil that beginnings herald. They require the wide-eyed optimism of novelty, of a story whose end you do not yet know, and an open road in the early morning, quivering with excitement.

I

Prima Facie

1.

There's a halo around my eyes like I'm looking through the bottom of a beer bottle and the lights in the courtroom's ceiling are piercing. And I'm thinking of the South African runner, Oscar Pistorius.

Oh Oscar, your accent is just foreign enough to be exotic, and your notoriety for being notorious is as captivating as constipation that stretches out over days of meals that you cannot believe your stomach can make room for. The body, as French writers are always reminding us, is insistent in its pleas for attention.

2.

Some months ago, I hurt my knee falling, so I suppose that makes us brothers of a sort, Oscar. Your physique in the police photos of you standing on your amputated stumps, naked but for boxers, is far more impressive than mine has become of late, sagging under burdens and sloth and doing things while postponing other things to do. The way your body terminated suddenly below the knees made it seem as if you had been shortened, as if you were the subject of your own magic trick.

3.

What to do in Key West? While on the grand jury, during a break between cases—which is to say between bouts of listening to assistant district attorneys describe the ways others' lives had gone awry and deciding whether or not to indict—one of my fellow jurors told me he "partied, chased women," which I imagine is quite different from how Wallace Stevens spent his time there. When I think of Stevens on the beach, attempting to round out the order of sound, I picture him lily white and paunchy, wearing a wide-brimmed straw hat, his thin pale legs' flesh sticking from his shorts like the bare ends of Popsicles that have just been pulled from their wrappers.

4.

For years I felt the call of the beach like a vague, persistent longing, a yearning for shore and sky, a warm breeze that ruffles your hair, bare feet on the hot pavement as you walk back from the rented cabin after lunch and the sun high, high in the yellow sky, hanging like a beacon above the confectioner's cart. Then one day that longing left, and in its place I felt not so much as a hole as the impression of where a hole ought to have been. As if the hole had been dug in dry sand that immediately began spilling back down, erasing the person I used to be.

5.

I have never been drowned but can imagine it, the desperate gasp at the end that brings only water. Nor have I been shot but have heard that it feels, at first, like being punched very hard by a very hot fist. The witness testified that the bullet broke his femur as he ran so his leg wrapped around him like a snake, like rubber, briefly boneless in the moment before his inertia carried him forward onto the pavement. How, Oscar, do you think Reeva felt when your shots hit her body? Was there a moment when she felt the round that hit her head, before its edges opened like a flower?

6.

Upon impact, be it with a target or soft tissue, such as a hip or the side of a head, the bullet in question is designed to open its partitioned arms like the petals of a lily, to embrace its recipient. And then, by passing through their body with great violence (as the tips of its petals are sharp as razors), cleanse them of the sins of this world and prepare them for the next. Where I imagine the bathrooms are bright and clean and quiet, free of vermin and leftover shit, untroubled by the booming reverberations of toilets being flushed in poorly lit, cavernous bathrooms in which the tinny echoes of the central courtyard sound like transmissions from some mumbling god.

7.

But maybe, if we listen closely enough, we can suss out some manner of message in the radiators' subarachnoid gurgling, something that might help us parse the reams of peer-reviewed papers and protocols that threaten to multiply and spill off of desks and file cabinets and onto and then cover our floors and couch cushions and decorative plants. Though you may not seek it, life's effluvia will find you.

8.

One of the times I was miserable, when I was fifteen or sixteen, I can't remember exactly when but I do remember wearing a ringed t-shirt with a printed image of a Spam container on its front, when I was in Key West in my middle-teens with my family on a holiday in late July, when walking outside feels like being hit in the face by a sweaty armpit, we went to lunch one day, the same day we saw Hemingway's house, the one with the polydactyl cats, and when we had lunch at one of those ubiquitous outdoor grill/bar spots that are so popular in towns that largely exist to pour drinks, I ordered a lemonade and I'm certain that the waitress took pity on me and spiked it with vodka.

9.

As the walk away from the restaurant was a particularly bright one, and though it may have been the sun in my eyes, the world seemed lit from within, pulsing and blurred around its edges as seen through cheap drugstore reading glasses. The older I get the more my memories and fantasies intertwine, and I sometimes have difficulty recalling whether what I'm recalling is a memory or a fantasy or the memory of a fantasy. In college, when my sex-starved friend confessed to having a wet dream after dreaming about masturbating, my reaction was to laugh so hard I fell out of my chair. Now I like to think I'd be more sympathetic, recognizing the line between what we experience and what we dream is a thin one, if it exists at all.

10.

The difference being that in the morning, once the gears of the day have begun to grind, dreams tend to fade so that in their wake they leave only the merest whisper, like a stray hair against a cheek. Though reduced, those whispers of dream tend to linger, often far longer than do the memories of our actual experiences. I cannot really recall, for example, precisely how I reacted to the news of my father's death, but I do remember the feeling of feeling scooped out every morning for months after dreams at whose edges his presence lingered, like a half-forgotten athletic trainer standing behind the coaching staff on some game's sidelines, enveloped in a bubble of his silence of his own making that insulates him from the misplaced passion and vicarious aggression swirling around.

11.

The sound of the crowd sounded like the alternating murmur and roar of the sea. My father's voice managed to cut through the chaff, bothering me so tremendously that I paused by him on my run to defend the goal and, breathing heavily, told him to shut the hell up, much to the amusement of the other parents in attendance. What, Oscar, did the cheering crowds sound like to you? Did their roars fill your head until you could no longer hear the sound of your own thoughts? Hence the obsession with guns, with spending your free time on shooting ranges blasting targets in preparation for conflict with shadowy criminals in the violent, race-riven culture you call home?

12.

Between 2012 and 2013, there were 16,259 murders in South Africa, a rate of about 31 per 100,000 people. In 2013, there were 256 murders in Philadelphia, the city I call home and which feels like a family abattoir when I'm feeling guilty thinking of my mother's ashes interred beside my father's remains in a grave whose stone we've yet to get around to having inscribed. One of the 256 people murdered in Philadelphia in 2013 was Christian Massey, for refusing to give his headphones to his killer.

13.

Shot in the back after refusing to hand over his new headphones, Christian Massey was only twenty-one when he died. He was, by all accounts, a gentle giant of a human being, standing six feet two inches and weighing approximately 300 pounds. Christian Massey played several sports and was loved by all whose lives he touched. When I was twenty-one, I weighed little more than a leaf and was hardly gentle, at least in my attitude. I took pleasure in my own nastiness and biting, incisive snark and substance abuse, and I thought frequently, with a twisted sort of glee, of how my own suicide might serve to make more of an impact than had my life to that point; to pass the time, I would fantasize about my own funeral, basking in my mourners' cathartic wails and caterwauling expressions of grief. I wanted to die not because I was miserable but because I wanted others to be miserable on my behalf: I wanted to be their wellspring of regret and loneliness and public expressions of sympathy.

14.

In *Being and Nothingness*, Sartre writes "shame is shame of oneself before the Other," as the Other puts one in the position of passing "judgment on myself as on an object, for it is as an object that I appear to the Other." With which I have no quarrel but to point out that the word "object" could here be easily (and perhaps should be) replaced with "target," for what are we but targets for others to pin ribbons on, donkeys missing tails or that stack of unused crook cutouts waiting to be put up on the rack at the shooting range, the detective placing his right palm on his infrequently fired gun when he lowers his hand after being sworn in. But despite the reassurance it offers, as he sits the detective angles his body away from his weapon because it digs into his hip and his lower back aches on the hard wooden chairs and it is uncomfortable in the courtroom, outside of which and down the dim, meandering stairs, there are food trucks and the Parkway is lined with flags of all nations, black and yellow and green and white and red and blue flapping in the wind, now seen and then not, like memories in the morning of the previous night's half-remembered dreams. Hear Ye, Hear Ye, Hear Ye: All Rise.

Video, Videre

After waiting an appropriate interval—for the curtains to close, for the audience's applause at the last syllable of the play's last scene to wane long enough for the curtain to close and then open again and the cast to begin taking their bows to even louder, more sustained applause and cheers, during all of which we were sitting on the catwalk looking down the tops of our friends' and families' heads below, our feet dangling over the catwalk's edge as we held onto its railing, tethered by ropes and clips and welded steel—Matt eventually said *Now, go now, now now now* and out we went, off into space, rappelling down down down, the stage below rushing up to meet us.

*

I would not necessarily characterize what I felt about heights, up until I no longer felt the feeling I felt—more or less at the exact moment that I landed on the stage the night *Something Funny Happened on the Way to the Forum* closed—as *fear* per se, because to that point I'd not had enough experience of heights to fear them. Say *dislike* then: I had a dislike of heights. But it was stronger than a dislike, and not so strong to be considered a *loathing*, so maybe aversion? Detestation? Hostility toward? Disquietude? Yes, *disquietude*. Heights tended to place me in a state of disquietude.

Growing up in the relatively flat, soft-rolling-hills suburban mid-Atlantic, I wasn't presented with many opportunities to experience true heights, the sort that can be described as *dizzying*. Yes, there was the time we went to the top of the World Trade Center, and the many climbs up the winding lighthouse stairs in Cape May, NJ. And when I was ten or so, my father worked for a time, seemingly only at night, in what to me was a very shiny office building, and his own office was many stories up and looked out over a dark parking lot, and beyond the parking lot the expressway, and beyond that the river winding like a ribbon to the city, which shone on the horizon.

Rather, much of my life was spent no higher than homes' third floors, and far more frequently at ground level—on planed playing fields and on the floors of carpeted rooms, venturing to the creek down the street when the civilized, paved entertainments that normally sustained us grew thin. Heights, therefore, were a form of bogeyman: I experienced real heights and real vistas infrequently enough that they were rare and special and, like all rare, special things we encounter sporadically, somewhat terrifying. Their newness, and that they existed concurrently with the world with which I felt so familiar, scared me. Heights could kill me.

*

Seen from above, there seems to be little beach where California's Mattole River meets the Pacific Ocean. The transition from land to sea looks abrupt, as the summer's dry, yellow grass—maize and goldenrod, straw and cream—terminates in a band of green fed by the spreading delta created by the river's alliance with the sea. What beach there is is interrupted by the flow of the river itself, running parallel to the waves' rhythmic pleating before making a sharp left and heading to its source and terminus. The river flows fast and free, and the channel it cuts through the pebbled sand looks almost machine-carved. The sound of the ocean dominates, and here and there driftwood lies, bleached by salt and sun and looking like great knobby bones.

*

The word *vista,* "a view or prospect," comes to English directly from Italian's *la vista,* sight, view, vision, and yes, vista. That word, in turn, comes more or less unchanged from Latin's *video, videre,* to see (more accurately: I see, to see). The Latin word comes from a variety of older sources, including the Ancient Greek οἶδα, to know. This word is also related to the archaic form of *wit*, to know, rather than the modern sense of wit as humor. Hence the phrase "to wit": that is, to say.

Such an etymological progression shows an interesting, if obvious, connection: to see something is to gain some form of knowledge (about the thing seen, the world, one's place in the world vis-à-vis the thing seen). Moreover, following *to know*, to *to see*, to *vista* (which we often think of a pleasant thing), to gain knowledge of something is therefore pleasant, or at least enriching, as knowledge is at least enriching if not necessarily pleasant. And vice versa: experiencing a vista shows us more of the world, giving us knowledge that we heretofore may not have had.

*

Almost all hobbies, once one learns enough about them, are almost perversely complicated. Take cycling, for example: say one has recently begun to seriously enjoy riding one's bike and is interested in cycling more seriously. In addition to investing in a proper bike, one should, if one is to take one's new hobby seriously, acquaint oneself with all manner of mechanical and technical terms: front and rear derailleurs; dropouts; fork blades; crankset, crank, and pedal; the head tube, the seat tube, and the down tube; brake pads, brake cables, caliper and handles. Then there is cycling apparel, which is legion—shoes and helmet and padded shorts and tight moisture-wicking shirts with pockets at the small of the back, and on and on.

Likewise climbing. If anything, climbing is even more gear-oriented than cycling, even though the latter is an explicitly technological sport; one cannot cycle without a bike, but one can climb without climbing gear. To wit, a short list of climbing equipment: nuts, chocks, and cams; chalk and comfortable clothing; form-fitting shoes and/or crampons for climbing in winter; helmets; belaying devices and pulleys and rappel rings; carabiners and harnesses; and most of all, rope rope rope.

None of which I understood when Matt showed us how to put on our harnesses and attach ropes to our harnesses and eventually how to rappel down from the catwalk to the stage below, slowing our descent by wrapping the rope around our thigh and controlling the speed at which it let out, and therefore the rate at which we fell, by applying or releasing pressure. My first few trips down were slow and jerky, marked by hesitation. Thereafter they grew faster and faster, until I was nearly falling freely toward the floor, and of my own accord.

*

From Walt Whitman's *Leaves of Grass,* "A Farm Picture":

> Through the ample open door of the peaceful country barn,
> A sunlit pasture field with cattle and horses feeding,
> And haze and vista, and the far horizon fading away.

*

My introduction to what Whitman called California's "golden hills and hollows" and "flashing golden pageant" was not to its more absurd majesties—in its Central Valley, or up north, among groves of redwoods—but to its highways. My boss and I stayed in La Jolla because the hotels in San Diego were full, and so our mornings and evenings were spent among the great convoy of commuters on I-5— tractor trailers and school buses and motorcyclists drifting between lanes as if to defy Death. Nonetheless, the view from our rented car's passenger seat was a balm; I could feel my whole being being unraveled by the tremendous space that surrounded us, the ocean on one side and the stark road cut cliffs the other, and the big, boundless sky above all.

I had been indoors too much, and even when outdoors I felt as if New York's clutter was pressing down upon me like a great weight.

The subway let me off in the basement of my office building. My apartment's front windows faced east, our bedroom to the west; it was shaded on the west by a backyard of overgrown trees and the east by a school. While my office at the time was quite high up, on the ninth floor, from my window one could only see the windows of other buildings that surrounded my building like a fence. Some nights, after work let out, I would deliberately walk down Fifth Avenue, fighting the flow of crowds of shoppers and tourists making their way north, until I came to the intersection of 42nd street and the Public Library. For there, with Bryant Park's oasis to the east, the metropolis's looming valley is broken up by the trees growing in front the library like a reminder that where I stood was once (and will someday in the future again be) ruled by the earth beneath the concrete and subterranean plumbing and transport beneath my feet. The stone lions sitting vigil on the library's steps affirmed this for me, albeit silently.

*

In *My First Summer in the Sierra*, the naturalist John Muir writes of Yosemite National Park that the "whole landscape glows like a human face in a glory of enthusiasm, and the blue sky, pale around the horizon, bends peacefully down over all like one vast flower." The same could be said of Lassen Volcanic National Park, approximately 300 miles to the north/northwest of the far more famous Yosemite. Per the National Park Service, in 2013 427,409 people visited Lassen versus Yosemite's 3,691,191. Lassen is also much smaller: it contains 100,000 acres against Yosemite's roughly 750,000. But while Lassen may be small for a national park (by size, Lassen is the thirty-seventh largest, while Yosemite is the sixteenth, though Lassen's 100,000 acres is still enormous) and is relatively obscure, it is certainly extraordinarily beautiful. Mountains and valleys, colorful dunes, hot springs and, according to the National Park Service, "steaming fumaroles, meadows freckled with wildflowers, clear mountain lakes, and numerous volcanoes," oh my.

It is also home to the Cinder Cone, which is a literal cone of cinder. More specifically, it is a 700-foot-tall mound of scoria—volcanic rock—that grew around what is a now-dead volcano. From the top of the Cinder Cone—around which there winds a difficult trail, as the stone that makes up the cone is loose and shifts underfoot, especially if it is a windy day, in which case small stones are sometimes whipped against one's face as one trudges one's way to the top with tears in one's eyes—you can see much of Lassen's wonder.

To the Cinder Cone's immediate southeast lie the "Painted Dunes" and beyond them the "Fantastic Lava Beds." To its northeast is Butte Lake, and to the south Snag Lake and beyond that Juniper Lake and its little campground. From the eastern edge of Juniper Lake, standing among the beds of wildflowers—monkeyflowers and larkspurs and St. Johns wort and paintbrushes of every hue—if one looks almost directly west, one cannot help but see Lassen Peak looming over the entire area like some godhead. Standing more than 10,000 feet, Lassen dominates without attempting to do so, and while in its shadow, one is nearly always aware of its presence, the peak's sheer faces highlighted by a smattering of snow even in another long hot summer of too little water and drought warnings that cannot be shouted loud enough.

*

Driving directly into the sun, we climbed to the top of the high hill in Ali's jeep, all of us stuffed into the car like some advertisement for youth, with music, holding onto roll bars at every unseen boulder and dip in the hill's side, thinking we'd tumble over at any moment. From the top of the hill we looked down at the Mattole's mouth, and watched it open its lips lightly as it approached the Pacific's margin. To the north, a bank of cloud or fog hung over the high, hilled terrain through the middle of which the Mattole cut a minor canyon.

To the west, the hill dove sharply down in a cliff and while leaning, peering over, I thought about how it wasn't remarkable that I wasn't afraid of the cliff's height. I might have been afraid, once, before I learned that some falls are revelatory instead of fatal, but by that late afternoon above the Mattole I had fully assimilated my fear's absence. It wasn't remarkable that I wasn't afraid but it was liberating; had I been afraid I might have stayed in the car, with my eyes still shut from the lurching trip up. Instead I had the wind on my face and the sun on my side, an afternoon years later I still remember as if the taste of it had never left my mouth. And it never will, I hope.

Winter Landscape with a Bird Trap

For many years I pronounced the word juxtaposition *yuxtaposition,* with a y, thinking erroneously that the j was silent. Upon learning that the j was in fact pronounced, I was terribly embarrassed, because starting at a precociously young age I had said the word often, and was quite proud of my ability to use

juxtaposition, from the French and the Latin, its root *jugum, -i,* meaning "yoke," juxtaposition is the yoking together of (two) things in such a way that their being yoked together makes one ponder what possible connections they might have. Take for instance all the yoking going on in the great juxtaposer Pieter Brueghel the Elder's *Winter Landscape with a Bird Trap,*

1565: children ice skating and snowy houses and denuded trees and wind whipping across a cold sky and a brace of geese, a single crow, and on the right a lean-to bird trap leaning-to, sparrows playing about, the bird trap menacing in that it could, but has not yet, fall on and squish the sparrows playing in the melted dirt-darkened snow around the bird trap, O happy sparrows.

Say it with me: *yuxtaposition,* with a y!, pronounced in unconscious acknowledgement of the word's forbears, the possibility of death on the right side of Brueghel's painting highlighting all of the life filling the rest of the composition, the lean-to a nagging notice that somewhere probably right now your creditors are rubbing their pale clammy hands together in poorly lit silent rooms, drinking pot after pot of black coffee and blinking infrequently, cigarettes dangling from their lips as they pore over piles of legalese and addenda printed in black and white,

which colors are so much easier to make sense of than the world's interminable and nauseating grey tones, not to mention the omnipresent meta-color brown, which color is like that guy who wants to be your friend but you don't want to be his because he's a little weird and dresses like his wardrobe literally exploded onto his body, brown less a color than an amalgamation of compromise, a modestly paying administrative position at a Fortune 500 company, the kind of job that really makes you appreciate the end of the day and the first sip of your first drink at happy hour, for as they say in vino

in *Veritatis Splendor* relativism makes the acknowledgement of absolute truth impossible wrote Pope John Paul II, late of this life, for how can one acknowledge truth qua truth if one is caught up in the *but thises* and *what about thatses* of relativism, though one might argue in return that relativism does not necessarily, your Holiness, cast truth out of the house of the Lord but simply relegates it to its place, nigh untouchable and distant, like that unattainably hot girl at the party with the curves that have got to be seen to be believed

a ten to end all tens, and you in the corner sipping punch from a red plastic party cup furiously sending your gaze like a laser beam across the room to land like an index finger in the girl's cleavage, your eye-finger creeping into the gap between her breasts like that frozen lake and/or river that separates the houses lining the shore in Brueghel's painting, a church on the right, its steeple disappearing up into the cold sky behind the vascular branches of the tree directly above the bird trap, which is made of wood which fact is somehow perfect, for if you must kill why not do so with a tool made from a thing with which the thing you are going to kill once called home. Because

birds sit in trees, birds rest on trees' branches and call to one another, birds fly down from trees' branches to eat seeds scattered on the ground and then fly back up to place leaves or twigs in their nests, which, though made by creatures lacking opposable thumbs, are often marvelously round and surprisingly even of construction, formed in a

circle which has no real points of landing or departure and therefore no Manichean truths, no contrasts to point to and say, this thing is like this and that thing is like that, and the difference between this and that is that this is this and is not that. But a circle can't be defined by what it is not because a circle, cliché though it may be, lacks the right angles that muddle our endless masturbatory narcissistic searches for personal definitions of just what it is that is true and false.

For example. Have you ever noticed how when people ice skate they most often do so in circles and/or figure eights, in little imitations of Möbius strips, and boy does that make one wonder about why they do that, like maybe they glide on ice in circles not just because it's hard to turn sharply on ice skates but because rounded shapes are somehow more pure than angled ones in that circles are inherently infinite and therefore godlike, and angles remind one of roads and coming to complete stops at stop signs, an activity that arrests the very thing one is trying to do. Which in this case is to move forward, much like the skaters in Brueghel's piece: to skate down the frozen lake between the houses flanking the banks, smelling the smell of morning bread and wood smoke curdling out of chimneys into the crisp January air, your wool clothes heavy around your legs and chest, face numb, skating past the other children playing, past the bird trap on the hill on your right, past the dock to your left, past the boy in a boat on the ice, past and around the curve in the river until you reach the bridge at the end of town and, while stooping, use your hands to push the ice below you to move yourself forward, you emerge from under the bridge and come to the edge of the ice where, choosing your footing carefully, you step off of the ice into the frozen snow of the bank and

clump your way up the hill, through the trees, a murder of crows cawing with great clamor overhead, until you are on the hill beyond the town, and then you turn around so you can look back on the town and see the landscape you've just crossed, the distance rendering it smaller and more absurd (but also somehow more precious) than you remember it seeming as you passed through it, the houses looking less like the warm large structures they did when looming over the pond as you skated by than they do now, a tableau of domesticity, and then you exhale and the rich white rolling fog your hot breath creates hides everything from view, for a moment.

II

The Lump in Adam's Throat

1.

So the reason that uh we're here talking is cause I have some pretty heavy news, I guess, to uh say, unfortunately we're gonna have to cancel a bunch of our shows coming up and uh and

Of the three Beastie Boys, Adam Yauch's voice was always the most strained, rasping and hoarse; his delivery, even when delivering the softest of lines on studio recordings, sounds like he's been shouting for hours, and in the back of his throat you can hear congestion needing to be cleared, the sort of angry, rolling growl that children think their fathers cultivate intentionally, intimidating and low. In contrast to the whining, vaguely irritating needling of Ad Rock and Mike D's voices—whose voices really do beg the question of how these guys ever became so famous, the groundbreaking beats and sampling and whiteness in a world dominated by black rappers aside—Adam Yauch's (or MCA, as he was known on stage) comes across as an almost sotto voce response to the others members' piercing calls, a sort of shouted whisper that simultaneously excites and calms.

2.

actually push back our record release, um, cause recently, ah, about, well about two months ago I started feeling this little like lump in my throat like you would feel if you have uh swollen

The word hypochondria, which the Oxford Dictionaries define as an "abnormal anxiety about one's health, especially with an unwarranted fear that one has a serious disease," comes from the Greek *hypo*, under or below, and *chondros*, chest or breastbone or cartilage. Our sense of the word dates, in part, to English poet and playwright John Dryden's "An Evening's Love," from 1671, alternately titled "The Mock Astrologer." In this comedy, hypochondria is a sort of melancholy without cause, "a certain species of the Hysterical Diseases; or a certain motion, caused by a certain appetite, which at a certain time heaveth in her, like a certain motion of an Earthquake."

Ignoring the gendered (and possibly sexualized) implications of this definition of the word, further inquiry leads to the Ancient (Greek) hypochondria, which was the seat of the stomach and viscera and therefore the source of the low vapors and spirits that emanate from said regions; the belief was that sadness and melancholic feelings arose in the gut, under the breastbone. Sadness comes, so to speak, from a pit in one's stomach—which term for the depression between the ribs comes from the 1650s, and "abode of evil spirits" from the thirteenth century.

A hypochondriac, then, is a person afflicted with such a causeless melancholy, namely the melancholy of erroneously feeling afflicted with disease. The sort of person who should not be allowed to Google their symptoms, and whom doctors and EMTs might behind the patient's back call a "squirrel" or a "SARS," as in She Ain't Really Sick.

But the thing about hypochondria is that while diseases are complex and their diagnosis should really be left to the professionals, just enough information about diseases to make one paranoid is readily available. For example, these similar symptoms: The symptoms of the common cold and the flu and bacterial meningitis, the latter of which can kill you if left untreated, and even if discovered early kills up to ten percent of those who get it, are headache, fever, and a stiff neck, among other things. But what if one is prone to getting a stiff neck frequently anyhow, because one's pillows are too hard and that's just how one's stress manifests itself sometimes? How is one supposed to tell if the stiff neck combined with their fever is a run-of-the-mill cold plus a stiff neck or meningitis?

Likewise bacterial pneumonia, which starts out very flu-like (cough, fever, chest pains, headache and muscle aches, etc.) but can progress to a very serious condition very quickly. Jim Henson, of *The Muppets* and *Sesame Street* fame, died only four days after first complaining of his symptoms, of toxic shock syndrome brought on by the streptococcal bacteria that caused his pneumonia. If stuff like this can kill the creator of Kermit the Frog, what hope is there for the rest of us?

3.

glands you would feel if you have a cold so I didn't think it was anything, but um, but then just recently when we were over in Europe doing promotion I started to think I should talk to my

Released on the second Tuesday in July 1998, the Beastie Boys's *Hello Nasty* is one of those records that looms large in my life more because of the circumstances that surrounded my listening to it than because of how I actually felt about the album when it came out, or how I feel about it now. By the time *Hello Nasty* was released, the Beastie Boys had been together for almost as long as I'd been alive, and had been one of hip hop's most seminal acts since I was a small child; by the time *Hello Nasty* was released the Beasties had fully completed their metamorphosis from a punk group to a hip hop group to a pop version of a hip hop group. Which is not to say that I don't enjoy *Hello Nasty*: I do. Tremendously. But it's an uneven record. For every amazing track like "Body Movin'," there is a party-killer like "Sneakin' Out the Hospital." Though not a bad song per se, "Sneakin' Out the Hospital" interrupts the flow of the album much in the same way that interludes on many other rap albums do (see Ghostface Killah's otherwise excellent *The Pretty Toney Album* for a particularly skit-laden offender). Of *Hello Nasty*'s twenty-two songs, half lack the up-tempo urgency and fun that make so much of the Beastie Boys' discography enjoyable.

There's a party suite toward the beginning of the record—the "Just a Test," "Body Movin'" and "Intergalactic" combo—that really makes the record great and is what made it so popular, specifically "Intergalactic," an unconventional weirdo pop hit that features the chorus "intergalactic planetary / plan-a-tary, intergalactic." And this party suite was the soundtrack to the weekend in Sea Isle, on the New Jersey shore, that I spent with my then-girlfriend during the summer of '98, the summer following our graduation from high school. Or at least *Hello Nasty* seemed to be the soundtrack to that weekend of watching others drink cheap beer in the homes of my girlfriend's friends' aunts who were away for the week, as I heard the Beasties everywhere, and the party suite in question certainly has become since said soundtrack, as my memory of that summer and the experience of listening to *Hello Nasty* are forever intertwined. To evoke Proust, it is a pop-rap madeleine. But though I didn't know it at the time, that was my youth's ultimate summer.

Because for many of us white, privileged middle-class Americans who went to college immediately after high school, the summer following one's graduation from high school is marked by the transition to adulthood (insofar as being a freshman in college constitutes being an adult), and in my own case moving away from home for the first time, to live and go to school in a small town in Ohio where I knew no one. For me, it was a summer marked by freedom. Not really freedom from worry or apprehension, as I felt much of both, but freedom, briefly, from the expectation of schooling and indeed even from my friends and girlfriend. We all celebrated and went out and had as much fun as we could because we were all going our separate ways in several short weeks, and the alternative of being terribly sad about all that is rather unfathomable to eighteen-year-olds who feel they have their whole lives ahead of them and who have really begun to discover in an unfettered way the euphoria that being half-drunk brings the first handful of times one gets half-drunk.

So it doesn't really matter that my time in Sea Isle was a mixed bag—I did not lose my virginity but came close; I chickened out and refused to play flip cup; I learned that, at the time, I couldn't drink much; I was too scared to admit to my girlfriend's cousin that I couldn't operate a manual transmission and so turned down his offer to drive his Porsche, which I coveted; and most juvenile of all, I got my eyebrow pierced. My memories of that time still sound, if memories can have a sound, like the goofy bouncing tin drum island beat of "Body Movin'."

4.

doctor, and so I called my doctor and saw him when I got back, this was about two weeks ago, and he sent me to a specialist and they did tests and I actually have a form of cancer

When Adam Yauch died on Friday, May 4, 2012, in a room in New York Presbyterian Hospital, I was sitting in a large, somewhat stuffy conference room in Philadelphia listening, as intently as I could, to a series of presentations on genomic medicine: how genomic approaches (medicine that uses genomic information, i.e., information contained in genomes, i.e., the total sum of an organism's genetic information, to inform clinical care) might impact the future of medicine. Presentations were given on data management, on recent rare disease findings, using molecular data to diagnose and discover disease, and on the future directions of the whole field.

Because my scientific training consists of a few years of high school science classes in which I did middlingly and the bare minimum of undergraduate courses, suffice it to say I had a hard time following said genomic presentations. While at Kenyon College, I took ethology and psychology to satisfy my math and science requirements, barely passing both courses. And when looking at colleges during high school, a major stipulation of my search was that none of the schools I considered would have strict math and science requirements, as I was terrible and uninterested in both. It was only natural, then, in the perverse logic of dysfunction that has defined my adult life, that after years of artistic and literary training I would find myself a sort of science writer, Googling almost every term of every assignment I was given, with a well-thumbed high school science textbook on my desk.

But one cannot look up words as quickly as one hears them, so the morning in question—when I was barely two months into a job in which I felt somewhat out of place but dammit, it was a paying job and I'd *needed* one of those—I did my best to follow what the various PhDs and MDs and laboratory directors and principle investigators were saying, to little avail. Most of that morning felt like I was stuck inside one of the Charlie Brown movies, listening to Charlie's parents' wah-wah pedal voices drone on. I fiddled with my phone.

And while distracting myself, I saw the news that MCA had died. Forty-seven years old at the time of his death, Yauch died around 9:00 a.m., presumably surrounded by those friends and family who were able to make it to the hospital and who were allowed to visit him, visitation rules being what they are. He was probably hooked up to a variety of machines—various IV lines running from his body to infusion pumps, his heart and respiration monitored; he may have even been catheterized—but my guess is that his death on that warm morning was not expected, as he might have otherwise been at home. Who knows; he could have been in the hospital for treatment, maybe another round of radiation, and when his doctors noticed something awry, he was admitted, and while in the hospital things went south very quickly, so much so that his wife was on the phone all night long and into the creaking, bleary hours of the morning frantically telling everyone she could reach how *you'd better get up here this is it* and then, while Yauch's doctors and nurses moved in a maelstrom of activity, with the breath caught in the their throats they watched the ECG line go flat and the alarms went off and out faded the song of his life.

5.

in the gland that's over here, and it's actually, it's in a gland called the parotid gland and it's also in a lymph node right in that area so I'm actually gonna have to have surgery probably next week coming up, and um, and then after that have to have some radiation done localized in that area

The largest type of salivary gland, our parotid glands are located by each of our ears, extending roughly from the root of the ear's helix down below the lower jaw. Most salivary cancers, according to the National Cancer Institute, begin in the parotid gland (as opposed to the sublingual and submandibular glands), andand this form of cancer, one emanating from the parotid gland, is what killed the musician Adam Yauch.

Again per the NCI, salivary cancers are rare and often present as painless lumps or difficulty swallowing or opening one's jaw very wide, also fluid in the ear or facial numbness. Adam, in the video that supplied this essay's section headers, said in 2009 he felt a "little like lump in my throat" that persisted for a while before he thought to call his doctor. Though the details have not been made public, my poorly educated guess is that upon diagnosis his cancer was stage II or early stage III, with minimal metastasization. Regardless, the treatment options for both stages include surgery followed by radiation followed possibly by chemotherapy in the case of more serious disease. According to the American Cancer Society, five-year survival rates associated with salivary cancer range from about 39 to 90 percent, for those that have and have not, respectively, spread far from the gland in question.

The surgery associated with salivary gland cancers is not a big deal, as surgeries go, but in cases where all does not go as planned the lower jaw may have to be removed. As was the case when it came to the film critic Roger Ebert's salivary and thyroid cancer treatment: Ebert lived without a fucking lower jaw, and the ability to talk or eat, for something like seven fucking years, which, forgive all the fuckings, is fucking crazy. Luckily, not so for Yauch. In an email sent to his fans following his surgery, Adam wrote (lack of capitalization his), "my neck and jaw are still pretty stiff from the surgery, but it gets better everyday ... but no sooner am i on the mend from this first torture than are they lining up the next one. the next line of treatment will be radiation. that involves blasting you with some kind of beam for a few minutes a day, 5 days a week, for about 7 weeks. that will start in a few weeks..."

Cancers of the parotid gland are an active area of investigation, assuming my search of PubMed is in any way indicative of the state of the field. Searching for "parotid gland cancer" returns over 11,000 results, including 2416 papers published between the beginning of 2010 and August 2016. One of these, published in *Annals of Maxillofacial Surgery*, is "Epithelial-myoepithelial carcinoma of the parotid gland: Clinicopathological aspect, diagnosis and surgical consideration." The study, written by three surgeons from the unbelievably picturesque northeastern Italian city of Udine, is a case study of a "42-year-old female patient who presented ... with a 6-month history of a painless swelling in the region of the right parotid gland." The paper includes a nauseating image of a "partial superficial parotidectomy," barely anonymized images of the patient before and after said nauseating, gruesome, gore-by-ear procedure, and several extremely long, unbroken paragraphs of obtuse medical speak, peppered with phrases like "Immunohistochemical evaluation revealed positivity for CKAE1/AE3 and CK7 in the small cuboidal, epithelial eosinophilic cells surrounding luminal spaces, arranged in ductal structures," and "There was some confusion between the terms EMC and adenomyoepithelioma because the neoplasm in the salivary glands has the same morphology as its breast counterpart." It also contains just enough information to reinforce my paranoia.

Because who knows, what if what one thinks is just a swollen lymph node, and that the swelling will go away on its own, or at least will go away on its own, or at least will go away as soon as one stops thinking constantly about it, is not a swollen lymph node at all but a "low-grade malignant neoplasm"? Ignorance, particularly ignorance of mostly rare but occasionally deadly medical conditions that initially manifest as the sort of harmless everyday physical hiccups we all experience more and more frequently as we age, is bliss. But the information to feed our fears is out there and accessible; all one needs to do is reach out and grab it. None of the above, for example, required any special access or knowledge on my part. I simply know what PubMed is—a free National Institutes of Health / National Library of Medicine resource that provides access to millions of biomedical papers and publications—and how to filter searches, something any fool familiar with Google can do. The same goes for so much other paranoia-inducing information: crime statistics associated with one's neighborhood; the origin and nutritional viability of those long, unpronounceable chemical ingredients listed on the side of one's box of breakfast pastries; vehicle-related deaths per year; and images, oh god, images: of hemorrhagic fevers, of what happens when high-caliber rounds hit human bodies; of plane crashes; and of one's exes looking older and puffier than one's memories of them, thus realigning our view of ourselves and the constantly crumbling world of jowls and cellulite, beer bellies and receding hairlines.

6.

but the good news is that it's um, that it is, that they did scans of my whole body and it's only localized in this one area and it's not in a place that affects my voice so that's nice ... that's convenient, so anyway, it's a bit of a, a little bit of a setback it's a pain in the ass

For several weeks during the fall of 2012, I felt a distinct tightness or ache in my chest, around my solar plexus, especially at night when in bed. At the time I told myself that it was nothing, that it was probably just stress, and I had good reason to think this was the case: my wife was unexpectedly pregnant, and I was working two jobs to make ends meet while she finished her dissertation and looked for work. Surely this is just all of the running around and juggling different responsibilities, I told myself. Surely it's just heartburn, I told myself, as I guzzled Maalox and popped antacids by the handful. But the feeling persisted, to the point that I occasionally felt short of breath and even sometimes felt my heart pounding through my chest, especially if I ran to catch a bus or climbed stairs too quickly. I began to become convinced that what was wrong with me was not gastrointestinal but cardiac; after all, I did drink, had in the past smoked, and had a vague family history of cardiac issues—my uncle had some ill-defined condition that prevented his drinking anything stronger than wine for years, and as a kid I'd had a heart murmur. So those nights, lying in bed, feeding my paranoia with books like Gunther's *Death Be Not Proud*, I thought wild, distracted thoughts: What if I have a heart attack? What will become of my wife and baby? Will it hurt? Am I ready to die? Oh god, what if I'm going to die of a heart attack, I'm only in my mid-thirties? I don't want to die of a heart attack. Will I?

Loath as I was do so, eventually I called my doctor. Despite my reluctance—borne out of having had to go to various doctors far too often as a kid plus a growing sense of my own mortality—my physician was perfect for paranoid, medicine-averse neurotic minor hypochondriacs like myself. An amusing, gentle Filipino guy, he seemed to have taken as inspiration for his bedside manner small-time comics' acts: his examinations are punctuated by wry observations and corny jokes.

So I told my doctor how I'd been feeling and he told me a funny story about how he still hadn't caught up on the sleep he lost the night before his first son was born, some sixteen or so years ago, and he listened to my heart and lungs and then pronounced me healthy. But he also recommended I go and see a gastroenterologist to be safe.

Who, when I eventually saw him, was not a funny warm Filipino generalist but a gruff, dour older Greek doctor, who terrified me. After we spoke—during which conversation I revealed my family history of colon cancer—he had me lie down on an examination table while he felt my stomach. He rather quickly diagnosed me with GERD, or gastroesophageal reflux disease. Also known as heartburn, which is no big deal and what I'd suspected in the first place. After said pronouncement, we capped off my visit to his office with a free rectal examination, because I'd been stupid enough to tell a gastro-enterologist that I had a family history of colon cancer. Then I went back to work.

In all, a mixed bag of a day. The ending fell flat, and more work could have been done in the description of the day's main body and hypochondriac, cancer-fearing climax to prepare readers for its denouement, two specialist's fingers several knuckles deep in the nar-rator's asshole. B-.

7.

but this is something that's very treatable in most cases, uh, it's, um they're able to completely get rid of it and people don't have continuing problems with it and uh, and they've caught it early and it's not anywhere else in my body

A confession: Whenever artists die, especially younger artists, I inev-itably look up their age so that I can compare my own progression as an artist to theirs. When the writer David Foster Wallace hung himself at forty-six-years-old in 2008, I was twenty-eight. Lots of time between forty-six and twenty-eight. Okay, I've got time. But people like the artist Margaret Kilgallen, who died at thirty-three in 2001, give me the chills. At thirty-three she'd had many shows, and there was even an *Art21: Art in the Twenty-First Century* segment devoted to the graffiti-evolved work she and her husband Barry McGee were doing in the Bay Area. What have I, who only moved to writing after I figured out that I wasn't much of a visual artist, done by age thirty-six versus all that Kilgallen did by the time of her death at thirty-three? Were I to drop dead now, at the conclusion of this sentence, would someone create a Wikipedia page in my memory? I doubt it.

Likewise, Adam Yauch. Though I've never had any musical aspirations (aside from vague guitar-god fantasies when a teenager), and I've certainly never wanted or tried to be a rapper, Yauch's death at forty-seven filled me with the same sort of existential dread and/or jealous loathing for others/myself. Not only was Yauch successful and rich, he was *wildly* successful and extremely interesting. Before the Beastie Boys became one of the most successful and influential music groups in the history of hip-hop, they were a punk band; the Beastie Boys's progression from punk to irreverent, genre-bending rap to massively popular yet still independent musicians should be a model for any artist looking to make a career and life of their art. Moreover, Yauch was a massively interesting, engaged dude: he was a loud pro-Tibetan freedom voice, a practicing Buddhist, and he founded a film company that helped produce and distribute artistically sensitive movies and documentaries. When Yauch died I was thirty-two, which means the next fifteen years of my life from that point had better be productive.

Perhaps it's kind of insane to judge one's worth against the accomplishments of others, particularly famous ones whom one does not know. Maybe Kilgallen was a terrible person in private; maybe she tortured small animals for fun. Maybe Yauch kept a small child in his basement, chained to the water heater. But the point is that our heroes are ideals, and one measures oneself against and admires ideals, not realistic appraisals. Children do not aspire to become middle managers: they want to be astronauts or Michael Jordan. And the death of our heroes seals both them and their accomplishments: once dead, our heroes can't be anything other than our heroes. Death frees them of the ability to disappoint us, either through their art or lives. They are ossified.

8.

so that's the good news.

But Adam Yauch isn't dead, not really. In fact, Adam Yauch will never die. Because Yauch was an artist (as all artists' lives and their art are forever intertwined, even more so after they die)—especially because he was an audio artist—his voice will live on as long as the innumerable copies of recordings of it also live on. In fact, as I write this sentence I can listen to Yauch rap right through my earphones, filling my head with the sound of his voice. I know that what I am hearing is not Yauch himself, but a recording of his voice, which is really only sound waves, which themselves are only vibrations that fall within a range of frequencies that humans' ears can catch and their brains can interpret as MCA trading lines with Ad-Rock on *Paul's Boutique*'s "Get on the Mic," Yauch delivering his lines in that hoarse whisper of his that will live on, assuming the gods aren't altogether uncaring, Yauch's voice will live on until Earth is a hot ball of irradiated pollution and the humans are long gone, cancer having eaten our bones' marrow and the roaches that rule the mess we've left behind having finished the job, and even then Yauch and his voice won't die, carried as his voice is by radio waves and television signals out into the cosmos, passing the asteroid belt that rings our solar system with nary a look behind its shoulder at the luminescent blue planet it left behind because, as the verse continues into the cosmos, there will always be new worlds to conquer.

Some Kind of Wunderkammer

Wunder ['vunder], *n.* (—**s**, *pl.* —) marvel, wonder, miracle
Kammer ['kamer], *f.* (—, *pl.* —**n**) chamber, small room

Pox Blankets, Pox Blankets, Come and Get Your Pox Blankets

Almost as varied as the tapestry of life—with sights to see; foods to eat; sensations to sense; the first thirty seconds of "Jesu Christe - Cum Spirito Sancto," from Mozart's *Great Mass in C minor*; the profusion of surprise endemic to the human race; the great Earth itself, verdant and green; and space that surrounds all, stars and nebulous black holes and meteors plunging through clouds of gas floating across an endless maw stretching out beyond imagination—are the ways we can depart this world. Death has many faces.

And death seemed to possess an especially varied variety of faces prior to the Enlightenment. For example, in seventeenth century Europe life was, as Hobbes said of man's "natural state" in *Leviathan* (1651), "solitary, poor, nasty, brutish, and short." But people living in seventeenth century Europe didn't live in some sort of so-called natural state, a mythical, rules-free wilderness of huddling over brush fires; they lived in the (also so-called) civilized world of kings and their counselors and the dirty, tired, poor masses the kings lorded over.

Life expectancy in seventeenth century Europe was roughly forty years. However, if you made it to thirty, which most people didn't, your life expectancy jumped to fifty-nine.[1] Amazingly, *half* of all people died before they turned twenty. Of those, between twelve and twenty-five percent died while infants. This contrasts starkly with the way things stand today, at least in wealthy countries. According to the Central Intelligence Agency's The World Factbook's 2015 estimates,

---

1   For this group, midlife crises must have come at about 29.5, which seems accurate.

life expectancy at birth in the United States is currently 79.68 years. The current world leader is miniscule, live-in casino Monaco, with a life expectancy of 89.52 years; last on the CIA's list is the central African nation of Chad, with an average life expectancy of 49.81 years.

In seventeenth century Europe, when one got sick one was generally in pretty dire straits. Pre-Enlightenment medicine was suspect at best, and at its worst contrary to good health. Much medical care at the time remained influenced by the writings of Cladius Galenus, a second century Roman physician who, while full of good ideas for his time, advocated now-discredited practices such venesection via pointy objects and/or leeches, to rid the body of foul humours and biles. And following the mantra of 'when in doubt, poop it out,' laxatives were also a common solution to physical ailments. Common causes of death in seventeenth century Europe included tetanus, diarrhea, thrush, whooping cough, diphtheria, dysentery, tuberculosis, typhus, rickets, scarlet fever, smallpox, and plague. Not to mention death by violence, through the usual ways: falling tree limbs, farming mishaps, construction accidents, warfare, and murder most foul. Death by many of the above diseases involved loss of fluids—especially dysentery—thus making being bled or health-by-laxative doubly harmful.

In sum, being sick in seventeenth century Europe = no good, in part because seventeenth century medicine = not very good. However, somewhat contradictorily, this also was a time of rapid technological and geographic progress, with new lands being "discovered" by increasingly advanced Western nations, with those new lands being subsequently plundered and their people put to the sword. Indeed, the period from roughly the end of the 1400s to the 1600s is known as the Age of Discovery, or the Age of Exploration or, as one might call it, the Age of Church-Sanctioned Conquest, and those two centuries saw a number of European nations—led in the main by Portugal—expand their territory and influence globally while also decimating several ancient empires and laying the foundations for future world powers, all with the backing of the Divine Providence.

Or at least with the backing of the Catholic Church. For example, in 1452 Pope Nicholas V issued his *Dum Diversas* ("Until Different"), which granted Alfonso V, king of Portugal and the Algarves, a wide array of colonial powers, including the:

> … full and free power, through the Apostolic authority by this edict, to invade, conquer, fight, subjugate the Saracens and pagans, and other infidels and other enemies of Christ, and wherever established their Kingdoms, Duchies, Royal Palaces, Principalities and other dominions, lands, places, estates, camps and any other possessions, mobile and immobile goods found in all these places and held in whatever name, and held and possessed by the same Saracens, Pagans, infidels, and the enemies of Christ, also realms, duchies, royal palaces, principalities and other dominions, lands, places, estates, camps, possessions of the king or prince or of the kings or princes, and to lead their persons in perpetual servitude …

In short, His Holiness the Pope granted the king of Portugal and by extension, other Western, Catholic kings in Rome's favor, the authority to conquer "infidels and other enemies of Christ" and thereafter keep them "in perpetual servitude." With this and similar edicts, the conquerors' moral fetters came off entirely, and the next several hundred years saw a progression of discovery, conquest, and massacre (often in that order). In 1492 Columbus landed in what is now the Bahamas, thereafter enslaving many. Hernando Cortes arrived on the Yucatan peninsula in 1519; Cortes would later go on to more or less exterminate the Aztecs. And on and on.

WONDER, WEALTH, AND MEMENTO MORI

This same period, the sixteenth and seventeenth centuries, also saw the rise of the "cabinet of curiosities," also called a chamber of curiosities or, in German, *wunderkammer* (plural *wunderkammern*), literally wonder-room or rooms. These cabinets, or chambers—and they could be both, sometimes being cabinets kept in special chambers designed for keeping those cabinets—were what they sound like: collections of wonderful and rare objects. These included works of art, relics from brutish civilizations[2], natural objects such as shells and horns, and the skins and stuffed heads of various colorful and deceased wild animals. These collections, which were kept exclusively by the wealthy, served much the same purpose that any collection of items serves: to show off the collector's knowledge of a subject while partially fulfilling his need to own all of that which he collects. But in this case, because these were collections of things that made up the world, and in particular the savage worlds, the possession of such a collection showed that its owner had, to some extent at least, mastered that world. In effect, they were private museums[3]. Consider, reader, the extreme difficulty, not to mention the resources, not to mention the hubris, required to create one's own museum.

One of the best exhibits in the Walters Art Museum, located in Baltimore's picturesque Mount Vernon neighborhood, is a recreation of a *wunderkammer*, which the museum calls "an authentic re-creation of a chamber of wonders" that suggests "a collection that might have been the pride of a sophisticated nobleman in the Spanish Netherlands (present-day Belgium)." The collection of objects contained therein is indeed wondrous, and is roughly indicative of the sort of collection a seventeenth century European noble might have put together. The depth and breadth of the collection in the Walters's *wunderkammer* also gives one a sense of just how difficult it might have been to put together such a chamber. Objects in the Walters's *wunderkammer* include:

---

2   See above re: conquest.

3   Indeed, several wunderkammern later became museums in their own right: note the profusion of items donated by private donors in the British Museum. And for a more recent example, visit Philadelphia's Mütter Museum, which prides itself on being "America's finest museum of medical history."

- A Chinese porcelain winepot, circa 1600
- A Chinese dish with dragons
- A Ceylonese ivory cabinet
- Various "Indian idols"
- An Aztec idol taken from Tenochtitlan
- An array of arrowheads
- A pop-eyed Panamanian frog pendant, made of beaten gold and copper
- A motorized silver wine decanter carved in the shape of the Greek goddess Diana, on a stag
- Geological wonders: crystals, amethysts, emeralds, rubies, and volcanic rocks
- A crocodile skull
- A stuffed "Brazilian hedgehog"
- A stag beetle, a flower beetle, and a stink bug
- A Japanese walking leaf and a Javanese stick insect
- Scarabs and scarab amulets
- Butterflies and moths
- A leopard skin
- A tortoise shell
- Various antlers
- A horseshoe crab shell
- The mummy of a young Egyptian girl, dating to between 100 B.C. and 100 A.D.

What we have are human wonders, occidental and oriental; examples of European ingenuity; geological extravaganza; faunal and entomical delights; the skulls and skins of beasts of sea and land; and an actual mummy, from roughly two thousand years ago.

But what was the appeal of these *wunderkammern*, and of the urge to collect such disparate objects? My guess is that the appeal lies in the ongoing search for a pleasant surprise, *eine angenehme Überraschung*, for when one's life is limned by unpleasant surprises so frequent that their surprise in time becomes less surprising than expected, and the increasingly infrequent gaps between periods of woe and decrepitude, personal or otherwise, begin to seem more like the exception to the rule of living rather than the other way around, that which is pleasantly surprising can restore, if only momentarily, some small vestige of the wonder and fascination with living that seems to dissipate by imperceptible degrees as one's youth fades. I can see it now: a slightly dandyish German or Belgian nobleman, in his late forties or early fifties, smelling faintly of brandy and quince, enters his *wunderkammer* and, while looking at his collection of shiny, colorful beetles from New Holland[4] or Van Diemen's Land[5], is able to forget momentarily about that nagging pain in his gut, and whether his wife knows that he has been sleeping with her maid, and that his son is a ne'er-do-well cardsharp, while concurrently being reminded—by looking at the beetles' Technicolor carapaces, procured at great cost—that he, our nobleman, is a successful, privileged man of the world, and the envy of his peers, his paunch and thinning hair be damned.

Of course, one cannot forget that curating a personal *wunderkammer* was an activity only available to the richest merchant princes and actual princes of the seventeenth century European world. And one cannot therefore forget that those people, these Rockefeller-Buffett-Koch forbears, need not have resorted to exotic collections of bugs and skulls to make themselves feel better about the fact that they lived in a world where people died young and were often underfed and disease was ever-present[6]: they were rich enough to receive the best medical care available, and lived in the most comfortable houses, eating the richest foods. Classism aside, just because the lives of the rich may be easy compared to those of the poor, wealth does not protect one against tragedy. While being well-off may mean that one's chances of contracting dysentery from drinking foul water, or getting

---

4   Brazil.

5   Tasmania.

6   Because this is still true to a large extent.

scurvy because one cannot afford to buy fresh food, are lower, no wall of money, no matter how high, can protect one from death and the grief that death brings with it. As the saying goes, no one gets out alive.

The appeal of amassing such a collection could, somewhat conversely, have been similar to the modern urge to relentlessly document our lives through photography (and to a lesser extent, video)[7]. Putting together a *wunderkammer* of one's own could have served a similar purpose: to package our lives in an easily accessible way, one that allows for revisiting at will. To paraphrase Stéphane Mallarmé, maybe everything in the world exists in order to end up in a collection[8] for, once collected, packed into a room or cabinet, and given a handsome label, the world is that much easier to comprehend. The items in a wonder cabinet are real, concrete things that their viewer can much more easily apprehend than the abstract folderol and tragedies that make up so much of life. For example, the pop-eyed Panamanian frog pendant in the Walters Art Museum's collection—dating to either before or during the early part of the Spanish conquest, 800-1521— has a double-headed snake in its mouth, accented by fine line work and spirals, which must have been almost inconceivably difficult to create, given that the whole pendant is only four and a half inches long and the snake in question but a fraction of that. The frog itself is a miracle, with its humps and depressions reflecting the light shining off the gold-copper alloy like the sun suddenly topping a distant hill at sunrise, bathing the land below in golden illumination like Apollo's hair cascading across his shoulders as he leans out of his chariot to caress your brow, the god's hand warm and fresh and smelling faintly

---

7   And, following this, share those photographs and videos (be they self-recorded protest videos or pictures of one's cats) through the instantaneous distribution system that is the Internet.

8   The original quote is "Everything in the world exists in order to end up as a book." Susan Sontag, for her part, changed this to "everything exists to end in a photograph" in her 1977 book *On Photography*.

of cloves. Who wouldn't rather spend their afternoon gazing at such an object than visit the doctor, or pay their bills, or look upon their sallow, lumpy reflection in the mirror?

MISE EN ABYME[9]

Also in the Walters's *wunderkammer* is a painting of a *wunderkammer*. Namely, Hieronymus Francken II and Jan Brueghel the Elder's *The Archdukes Albert and Isabella Visiting a Collector's Cabinet*, 1621–23. The title describes the painting's subject: The Archduke Albert VII, son of the Holy Roman Emperor Maximilian II and member of the Habsburg family, and his wife Isabella Clara Eugenia, daughter of Philip II of Spain, who are visiting the collection of a collector and, surrounded by five dogs, two monkeys, and various courtiers, admire the collection's flowers, paintings, globes, instruments, sea shells, and other curios. That this painting, which is of people admiring a *wunderkammer,* hangs in a modern recreation of a *wunderkammer* could not be more perfect. In addition to producing a mirror-within-a-mirror effect, the painting encapsulates the beauty, absurdity, lunacy, and tragedy akin to the Sisyphean task of collecting some of the world's most curious objects. It also acts as a convenient punctuation mark to any essay attempting to point out the connection between the rise of collections of this sort and living in a world where most people, wealthy and poor, often died young and sick: the Archduke in question, for all of his wealth, was sixty-one when he died. His wife made it to sixty-seven. Yet on they live in this painting which, due both to its quality and being partly painted by the famous Jan Brueghel the Elder (he handled the flowers; he died at fifty-seven, in 1625), will likely be carefully preserved for many years to come. Isabella and Ferdinand and their friends and their pets are lucky, not

---

9   "Placed in an abyss." More simply, when an image contains an image of itself, recursively.

just because they have been preserved at their height of their wealth and power, but because they have escaped the kingdom of death. They are safe beyond its walls, safe to forever endlessly visit this collection of curiosities and wonder and to have the collection's curator detail its contents to them, his mustache twitching with excitement.

Moreover, in the painting they are forever preserved in the moment of wonder (or at least in a moment leading up to wonder), which is like the orgasm's *le petit mort* insofar as while experiencing true fascination with say, a narwhal's pirouetting horn carried down across the arctic ice and frozen seas to reside in the warm sunlit room in which you now find yourself, you step outside life's cares for a moment and merely experience the languid moment of wonder as it crests around you. Only the slightly distracted, slightly worried look in Albert's and Isabella's eyes hint at the fact that they know they have made a narrow escape, for outside the walls of the painting Death paces back and forth endlessly like some emaciated guard dog, gnashing his teeth in frustration, for he knows, and Albert and Isabella know, that as long as they remain in this room, with its flower-perfumed air, they are beyond his reach.

Much Melancholy Stillness

Also known as Dirk, Dirck, Dierick and incongruously Thierry de Haarlem, the Netherlandish painter Dieric Bouts was born in either 1410 or 1420 and died in 1475, at the ripe old age of fifty-five or sixty-five, or somewhere in there: really, it doesn't matter, because if you lasted much more than a couple of decades in the fifteenth century, you were pretty old.

Dieric / Dirk / Thierry Bouts de Haarlem was an important and influential Northern Renaissance painter. Known for his figures' length and for their mournful, elongated faces, Bouts's characters have always struck me as possibly being less representative of the characters he is painting than of his own state of mind. That Bouts was working during a period in which European painters more or less *had* to paint religious subjects cannot be overlooked; if painters wanted to express themselves, they had to do so through the medium of painting religious subjects. With this in mind, Bouts's paintings, and all painting for that matter, can be seen as sorts of self-portraits. One cannot help but look at Bouts's characters' big sad eyes and gaunt features and wonder if Bouts himself was skinny and sad. Following this, in Bouts's work, there are media upon media. There is the medium of paint and brush, and there is the medium of the painting's subject matter, then there is the subject matter's subtext, and there is the wider world from which such subject matters and media are drawn. Ad infinitum, ad nauseam.

Aside from their starts and finishes and, if we're lucky, the particulars of a handful of business deals, we don't know much about the lives of many pre-modern Northern Renaissance painters. Bouts was probably born in Haarlem, and at some point in his early years made his way south, to Louvain, in what is now Belgium. I'm not sure why he did this; maybe Bouts traveled to Louvain to act as an apprentice, or maybe to follow his father, who may have been the landscape painter

Theodoric Bouts. Today, by car the drive from Haarlem to Louvain is a little over two hours, but this is the fifteenth century we're talking about, so, no cars. Though we can assume Bouts's family—let's imagine he traveled to Louvain with his family, for imagination's sake—wasn't poor, with his father being the possible painter that he possibly was, they almost certainly wouldn't have been overly wealthy, so they might have had to walk to Louvain. Or maybe they had horses, though they surely wouldn't have been able to afford enough horses to seat the whole family, so they would have likely crowded the whole clan into a slow horse-drawn wooden cart. I can see the scene now, the thin Dutch-Flemish people in strange hats, wearing tunics and hose, making their way across a blue and green landscape accented by canals and windmills, vast fields of tulips undulating in spring breezes.

Such a trip to Louvain from Haarlem would have taken about three days, plus overnight stays in whatever taverns or barns might have dotted the road. The trip, assuming it took place in the manner conjured, would have left quite an impression on young Dieric, despite the fact that he would have found Louvain to be similar to his hometown of Haarlem: both towns were walled affairs, defense-postured, Haarlem being on the River Spaarne, Louvain on the River Dijle. Unlike Haarlem, however, Louvain lies further inland (Haarlem is a mere five miles east of the North Sea), and Bouts surely would have noticed the change in the air and atmosphere as he and his family made their way south. Haarlem's elevation, like much of the Netherlands', is zero feet, while Louvain's is 114.

One cannot help but see reflections of such a trip's landscape in Bouts's work, as Bouts's paintings' backgrounds are often highly expansive, with rolling hills and rocky crags jutting from the earth, the misty watchtowers of distant cities, and often a lone tree or a copse of three or so trees reaching up into a sky deepening gradually into ever-darker shades of blue—baby blue to cerulean to navy, as if the land thinned and lightened the air which most closely surrounds it. Moreover, many of Bouts's scenes take place outdoors, often seemingly unnecessarily so. While a preponderance of vistas is characteristic of Northern Renaissance painting, Bouts's use of landscape is particularly insistent: his landscapes are so lush that they often overwhelm his painting's purported subjects. Sometimes one must move through a place in order to truly appreciate that place.

For example, Bouts's diptych *The Justice of Emperor Otto III* features landscape scenery in both its panels. On the left, we have the execution of a noble, which takes place just outside a city's walls, in what looks to be a clearing. The location strikes one as being the perfect place for a picnic. The painting's right panel shows an indoor scene—the aforementioned noble's wife pleading for justice—while just outside, filling the top left quadrant of the painting, we have an outdoor scene of the emperor's wife being burned at the stake. What's interesting about the latter scene is the way Bouts moves the viewer's eye up and away from the interior scene to the landscape outside, where the image of a woman being burned alive is less arresting than is the detail given to the hill on which her stake has been raised, the cityscape beyond, and a brilliant light-blue-to-dark-blue sky above.

Okay: Bouts moved. Okay. A lot of people move and always have, and in the fifteenth century artisans likely moved around often as their patrons changed, or were deposed, or were replaced by other rich people who had the money and inclination to support painters. Surely then, this move—which was only of 150 miles, no big deal, even by fifteenth century standards—can't be entirely responsible for the sadness which so pervades Bouts's work. Where else might it have come from? You, reader, can easily fill in the blanks with the myriad possibilities.

Whatever it was that happened, it certainly left its impression on Bouts. I can think of no other reason why Bouts's paintings are populated by such gloomy, dead-eyed sad sacks: he must be saying *something*. Take his triptych (a three-paneled painting) of *The Martyrdom of St. Erasmus*. Flanked on both sides by images of saints— Jerome (translator of the Bible into Latin) being on the left, Bernard (scholar-monk, instigator of the 2nd Crusade) on the right—the actual scene of the martyrdom is as fine an example of Bouts's droopy-eyed, dead-faced characters as you'll find.

St. Erasmus, born at some point in the third century, is less famous for his life and works than he is for the manner in which he died. Accounts vary, but supposedly Erasmus was beaten, befouled with excrement, thrown into a pit of serpents, had boiling oil tossed on him, enclosed in an inward-spiked barrel and rolled down a hill, had his teeth pulled out, was roasted, and had nails driven through his fingernails. Last but not least, as depicted in the painting in question, Erasmus was disemboweled. Per Bouts's painting, he was disemboweled slowly, while still alive: a small incision was made in his stomach and up through the incision his intestines were wound around a windlass and so out of his body. Altogether, one has over twenty-five feet of intestines in one's body.

Let's say you were to paint this scene, of a man being eviscerated. Wouldn't you paint it resplendent with gore and pain, with Erasmus's face contorted into a rictus of agony? You would surely use lots of red and pink and brown; the intestines in question would be shiny and slick with fresh blood. Above all, the image would be shocking and terrifying, because there's no way to get around the terrible violence that eviscerating a living person entails. One imagines, after all, that having one's entrails removed slowly (via a crank, no less, as if one's entrails were not entrails but were instead rope) would be so painful as to be unreal, and any image concerned with the depiction thereof should at least make an attempt to embody some of that terror and violence.

Bouts's painting takes a different approach. As Sir Joseph Arthur Crowe and Giovanni Battista Cavalcaselle say of another Bouts painting, *The Last Supper*, in their 1857 book *The Early Flemish Painters*, "[m]uch melancholy stillness pervades…" The same could be said for this painting. Erasmus lies naked but for a loincloth, bound only by the thinnest of ropes, on a wooden table at the center-bottom of the painting; his face looks less aggrieved than bored: certainly not the face one would think he'd be making. Most of the painting's characters' faces, in fact, share the same expression of blank boredom. Additionally, there is no blood or gore whatsoever. The only indication Erasmus is being disemboweled is the strange grayish string connecting his abdomen to the rod above him; were Erasmus not a grown man, one could almost confuse his intestines for an umbilical cord.

However, of extremely interesting note are the two men in the painting who *are* being affected by this gruesome scene: the two men working the intestines-removal crank. The man on the viewers' right—he of the orange tights, his crank at the apex of its cranking—looks vaguely down toward Erasmus's prone figure and bites his lip; the man on the left, his end of the crank at its base, the crown of his head hairless in a classic example of male-pattern baldness, he, he, well he looks downright distraught. Not only is his face suffused with sadness, guilt, empathy, what have you—his eyebrows are arched and his brow furrowed, and one can easily imagine him grimacing under that beard of his—but his body language also betrays his state of mind. Unlike the painting's other characters, the man-on-the-left-side-of-the-crank seems to be physically exerting himself. He is bending his knees into the effort of cranking, his thigh muscles bulge, and the way he is leaning far forward signifies not only that he is cranking an awkwardly designed crank but also that he might have put as much distance as possible between himself and the table on which a man is experiencing great, great pain.

The sad cranking man—who seems to be acting as the painting's conscience, and as Bouts's way of making a comment on just how terrible the subject of this painting is without resorting to the usual histrionics of extras beating their breasts or crying silently into their robes—looks as if he might spring away at any moment (and so too should the viewer), running wildly from the grisly business at hand into the verdant hills behind him. Because while bad things do happen, there are also hills in this world, and roads leading to the tops of those hills, from which vantage points one can, leaning against a tree, safe now, far from the horror, catch one's breath and, gazing over the valley below, dotted and patched with the multicolored quilted geometry of husbandry, see the other part of the world, the peaceful half, the one more seen but less often appreciated for its unassuming beauty: Oh look, the morning mist is just now beginning to burn off, look.

Jason Noble's Shoulder

I.

He said his shoulder had been hurting for a while, months in fact, and when his doctors took a look they found tumors spread across his body, a smattering of bad news leading to further bad news, grim conversations about surgery and which treatment option was the most effective and least toxic.

2.

"Efficacy" and "toxicity," to be specific, and "adverse events" versus "serious adverse events," patients plotted out by number and graphed according to progression-free survival and overall-survival and the definition of a complete response being a complete absence of cancer caused by treatment but that definition not extending to specify that the cancer need not be absent for very long to fit the definition of a complete response, therefore making it a term defined by what it means very narrowly and by transience and by the pyrrhic victory it implies.

3.

The musician Jason Noble was forty years old when he died, after three years of struggle, much of it publicly detailed on a blog that for years after his death remained up. For though we may die, those traces of ourselves we leave in the world, and more specifically on the Internet, often live on. Jason, whom I did not know personally but whose musical career I followed closely (though I only saw him perform in person once), died in the belly of the beast, so to speak, at the National Institutes of Health (NIH) in Bethesda, Md., unmistakable along Wisconsin Avenue (and Jones Bridge Road) for its sprawl and government-facility guard house and blast barriers. If the fight against cancer has a physical center, the NIH's headquarters in Bethesda are that center. In addition to conducting a tremendous amount of research of its own, the NIH is the "largest public funder of biomedical research in the world," according to its website. Of the many grants the NIH awards medical researchers, the R01—pronounced Are-Oh-One—is among the most coveted, granting as it does generous and lengthy support.

4.

Research takes time, time to explore diseases' "underpinnings" and to move work "from the bench to the bedside," often over the corpses of zebrafish and mice and monkeys and even the odd dog or cow or other "large animal model." Where, I've long wondered, do the bodies go? Are they moved from facilities at night, in red biohazard-emblazoned trash bags? Who takes them, and do they know what they do? But cancers like synovial sarcomas do not cure themselves, so sacrifices must be made.

5.

A cancer of the soft tissue, synovial sarcoma is rare, occurring in two to three per 100,000 people each year, which means that the chances that a specific musician hailing from grassy, whisky-soaked bellwether of clanging indie rock Louisville, Kentucky, would get synovial sarcoma are small. When I saw Jason perform it was with the modern classical group Rachel's (the apostrophe –s is not a typo), playing one cold night in Columbus alongside the electronic duo Matmos and if I remember correctly they played something from "Full on Night," the collaborative album they released together in 2000, the year we all thought was going to be the beginning of the end, Y2K having done us in.

6.

And what a beautiful performance it was, I think, though I can hardly remember now: the group's somewhat serious classical chamber music for rock fans contrasting nicely with Matmos's electronic eccentricity—this was during the phase when they were playing rat cages and using liposuction sounds to make dance music—and then both groups played together for awhile and I do recall tearing up, being, at twenty, prone to muffled and embarrassing public displays of emotion, as I was a goddamn mess.

7.

But was, for once, sober the night of the concert, which made the evening that much more significant, for the nights when I was sober that year had been eclipsed by the nights I was in no way sober, no indeed, as this was the year my roommate had had jaw surgery and his doctor had given him what seemed like an unending supply of Percodan with which to numb his pain. And my roommate, being a generous and giving friend, had helped me and many of our other friends numb all of our pain, both corporeal and spiritual; we discovered that if one took a Percodan and then drank several beers very quickly, one's pain would dissolve into an ether of floating softness.

8.

A combination of the opioid oxycodone and the analgesic aspirin, Percodan is sold by the Dublin, Ireland-based Endo International plc, and is classified as a Schedule II drug which group of drugs, according to the Drug Enforcement Agency, "are defined as drugs with a high potential for abuse," albeit "less abuse potential" than illegal Schedule I drugs like heroin and methamphetamine. Nonetheless, overuse of Schedule II drugs can potentially lead to "severe psychological or physical dependence." Percodan, per David Foster Wallace's term for certain substances from his novel *Infinite Jest*, is also "Too Much Fun," as the period of my life during which I took it fairly regularly was, I think, a ton of fun but hazy, marked by intoxication-caused disappointment and subsequent avoidance of disappointment via intoxication, which in turn led to other disappointments via responsibility-avoidance and therefore further attempts to not think about said disappointments via pharmaceuticals and alcohol and unconscious imitation of *Gone With the Wind*'s Scarlett O'Hara: Fiddle-dee-dee! I can't think about that today. I'll think about it tomorrow.

9.

Though the one Rachel's performance I saw in person was with Matmos, I prefer their *Music for Egon Schiele* to the collaborative *Full on Night*. Written to accompany a play about the early twentieth century Viennese expressionist Egon Schiele's life, *Music for Egon Schiele* is beautiful chamber music with highly present production. For example, on "Second Self-Portrait Series," the lead violin seems to almost take up a dwelling in one's head, particularly when listened to on headphones. In 1918, Schiele—who was ridiculously talented—died of tuberculosis at twenty-eight years, and the song is imbued with the gravitas and tragedy of that fact; the lead violin's heavy repeated notes seem, if one is in an interpretative mood, to resemble the forceful line work present in much of Schiele's art, which is composed to a large degree of bony figures with prominent cheekbones and hollow, sunken eyes looking at their viewers plaintively.

10.

Treated first, generally, by tumor resection followed by targeted radiation or, less targeted but often more effective, chemotherapy, synovial
sarcomas tend to progress to metastasis in several years and thereafter
to the increasingly diminished returns that fully metastasized tumors
bring, therapies tried and then discarded, one after another, until at
last a hospice bed is set up in the living room of one's family home
and the process becomes one of waiting, waiting, waiting. Unless, of
course, the cancer has already metastasized at the time of diagnosis, as
was Jason Noble's, in which case life's plot tends to move much more
quickly toward its resolution.

11.

*The first thing on our action list / Is to take your severed head down off the
shelf / Put it in a museum case*

The indie rock band The Shipping News's final album, the live-
release "One Less Heartless Left to Fear," opens with a shotgun blast,
the above lines from "Antebellum" more recited as if a mantra than
sung by Noble over a driving bass line and drum beat the number of
which I no longer know, my ability to read music having been lost in
the wistful fog that is my childhood: walking with what seemed an
enormous trombone to band practice in the sweltering summer of a
mostly shuttered public grade school littered with the prone carcasses
of cockroaches, always wishing I played the trumpet instead. Jason,
my own action list is much less dramatic, more concerned with bal-
ancing my tendency toward nostalgia with the need to be present in
the present, exercise versus sloth, daydreams against the insistence of
adult life's responsibilities, phone calls that need to be made and letters that must be mailed on time, in full.

12.

Before he was a founder and member of Rachel's and The Shipping News—which is named after the Pulitzer-winning E. Annie Proulx novel of the same name, the story of a sad man named Quoyle who moves to Newfoundland—Jason Noble was a member of Rodan, which was named after the Godzilla-universe pterosaur of the same name. Rodan (the band) only released one full-length record, 1994's *Rusty*, but boy is *Rusty* a doozy. The highlight of *Rusty* is undoubtedly the nearly twelve-minute "The Everyday World of Bodies," a jagged song of craggy peaks and valleys that uses repetition and multiple voices to lull its listeners into a stupor until the pounding last minute of the song, when the vocals are composed of variations on the refrain "I will be there / I will be there / I swear" until the song comes to a crashing halt where silence is once again king.

13.

Jason Noble was born in 1972 and died in 2012. Over the course of his illness—the first entry is dated September 3, 2009, and the final entry, an obituary, August 10, 2012—he and his wife and his family maintained a blog to keep interested parties up to date on his illness and treatment. They also opted to leave the blog public, so people like me (fans of Noble's work / irrepressible voyeurs) were also able to keep up on his illness and treatment. Which I did. Not religiously, but often enough that for more than two years checking Noble's blog became part of my normal internet routine: open browser, glance at *The New York Times*, look at email, look at *The Onion*, read Jason Noble's cancer blog, et cetera. During this same time period my mother was diagnosed with and succumbed to metastatic colorectal cancer and my mother-in-law was diagnosed with ovarian cancer and I was working on a manuscript of poems about cancer and I even took part in a fundraising walk, the Colon Cancer Alliance's Undy 500. Cancer, it seemed, was all around me.

14.

And I admit that I grew a bit obsessed with checking in on Noble. Not only was I concerned for the man's health—after all, he was responsible for several albums that I loved, and so was someone I looked up to in a vague way—but I also began to almost revel in the possibility that at any time the blog could contain bad news. Which is not to say that I wished him ill or that I wanted his condition to worsen. Hardly. But one does not tune into NASCAR hoping to see all of the cars run safely around the track until one is declared the victor: it is the possibility of disaster that draws us in. It is the possibility that bad things might happen to us but have not happened to us that makes rubbernecking at accidents on the highway so irresistible. Or, conversely, it is the very fact that terrible things have happened to us that makes confirming the fact that terrible things also happen to others so attractive, for witnessing others' tragedies makes us feel less alone in ours. Of course, none of this sort of navel-gazing narcissistic bullshit makes me feel any better. When I read that Noble had gone into cardiac arrest and died shortly after being accepted to a clinical trial—a trial he and his family were extremely excited about, for it offered real hope—I felt nothing but bad.

15.

Named for the flower it sprouts at full height, the scientific name of Kentucky bluegrass is *poa pratensis*. The flower itself is an understated thing, a dash of periwinkle reaching out from green shafts. But seen among its peers, in a prairie pasture of tall, blooming bluegrass, the flower is an exclamation of color hovering above and among a variegated field of green shoots in an eternally hot, buzzing summer of lazy flies and sweating glasses of lemonade on back decks and Jason brushing his dark hair back from his thin face thinking of the next line after the chorus, pen poised above a pad of legal paper.

Off to the west there seem to be clouds gathering and the wind has begun to pick up, rustling the pages of Jason's notebook and making the wind chime tinkle, chasing the felines indoors. It's time to go in, Jason. It's time to go in. Requiescat in pace.

III

Fuck You, Everybody

"You can turn the lights out. The paintings will carry their own fire."

—Clyfford Still

There's nothing like telling someone off. Particularly when the act is done explosively, at volume, when you're very angry; the telling off can be a release, letting all of the anger out of one's body like the popping of a water balloon. Indeed, that most cathartic of imperative phrases, *fuck you*, is a little bundle of satisfaction: the word *fuck* comes to a close as conclusively as any word in the English language, with its hard -ck, and *you* unequivocally directs *fuck's* action. Though logically problematic—the phrase could be interpreted positively, as *fuck* is slang for sexual intercourse, and telling someone to go sex themselves or be sexed is generally something that that someone might enjoy—*fuck you* has become the go-to expletival phrase in the English language. The gold standard of cusses, if you will.

But *fuck you* is hardly the only phrase in modern English to use the word *fuck*. *Fuck* is a truly versatile obscenity, able to be used, per above, to discuss sexual congress, or in a whole array of aggressive expressions. Just a few of the many, many examples: go *fuck* yourself; get *fucked*; *fuck* used adjectivally, as in *fucking*; *fuck* as a present participle; the present participle form of *fuck* used adjectivally, such as *that is fucking bullshit bro*; the word as jack-of-all-trades, *fuck you you fucking fuck*; and finally, used in caustic self-reflection, *fuck me I'm such a stupid fuck*. Of course, using any form of the word, especially saying *fuck you* to someone, regardless of whether or not you feel they deserve to be cussed out, isn't always a great idea, because *fuck*, in addition to being somewhat offensive (it is a "curse" word after all), can cut off conversation as suddenly as a slammed door, and one should take care when deciding which persons should and should not be told to go *fuck* themselves. *Fuck* is a giant heavy gold standard that can be dropped on others' heads, or on one's own feet.

*

Clyfford Still, abstract expressionist painter, asshole, genius, megalomaniacal egotist, and man who, in many ways, embodied the phrase *fuck you*, was born in 1904 in Grand Fork, North Dakota. Some 75.5 years later he expired, in New Windsor, Maryland, maybe because he smoked one too many cigarettes while working on his large, often oversized, abstract paintings of colors shearing their way up and down canvases like great serrated knives. That Still was born in a small city and died[10] in a small town—according to the 2010 Census, Grand Fork's population is roughly 55,000 while New Windsor's is just shy of 1400—is somehow appropriate, given the degree to which Still is said to have disliked and spurned his fellow man. His prickly, dismissive nature—Still famously hated the idea of selling out, and loathed the New York art world in particular— is legendary. For example, the former director of the San Francisco Museum of Modern Art, Henry T. Hopkins, is quoted in a 2007 *The New York Times* article as noting that when one visited Still:

> you weren't allowed to take a tape recorder or a notebook.
> You were just supposed to listen. He served you one cup
> of coffee, no seconds. He was like an avenging Protestant
> minister coming out of the barren lands of the Dakotas to
> the wicked city.

---

10   Still actually died in Baltimore, but close enough. One imagines that the time he spent in Baltimore at the end of his life, likely hooked up to some sort of medical equipment, was not significant. Terminally ill patients in hospice do not so much live in the place in which they are dying as exist therein.

Not that Still avoided society entirely, as during his life he lived in both the Bay Area as well as New York, among other large cities, but he certainly did return to something approximating his roots when he and his wife moved to New Windsor in 1961. I imagine he spent his last years stewing in his rage's juices, occasionally shaking his thin fists furiously at mirrors. Fuck you, everybody.

I can't remember when I first became infatuated with Clyfford Still's work, but I do remember the first time I saw a number of his paintings in one place. Because Still went to extreme lengths to control who could show his art, the Hirshhorn Museum in Washington, D.C. was, until very recently, one of the few U.S. museums to permanently house several Still paintings. Why? Because in his will Still specified that much of his work would only, and could only, be shown in a museum entirely devoted to his work. To wit:

> I give and bequeath all the remaining works of art executed by me in my collection to an American city that will agree to build or assign and maintain permanent quarters exclusively for these works of art and assure their physical survival with the explicit requirement that none of these works of art will be sold, given, or exchanged but are to be retained in the place described above exclusively assigned to them in perpetuity for exhibition and study.

Hence why, until the 2011 opening of the Clyfford Still Museum in Denver, Colorado, Still's work was largely spread out or shown in special shows. The Hirshhorn's Still paintings, much like those at the San Francisco Museum of Modern Art, are displayed together in their own room; I have always felt that walking into a Still room was akin to entering a cathedral. For the paintings are *large*. For example, *1948-C* (many of Still's paintings lack "proper titles" and sport year-appropriate labels in lieu of "untitled") is 80 ⅞ x 68 ¾ inches, or about 6 ¾ feet high by 5 ¾ feet wide. As much a painting as a piece of furniture.

*

What do I like so much about Still's work? Well, I could say the movement; I could say the way his paint is applied like plaster; I could say the way his colors seem to literally pop out of his backgrounds. Or I could point to how when I look at Still paintings my eyes tend to dart crazily around their surfaces, for the colors' vertical movements tend to thwart one's eyes' ability to see the paintings as wholes; maybe I could note how there is more going on, texture and visual-interest wise, in small sections of Still's work than there is in the entirety of many other painters' paintings' wholes. Arguments regarding technique and expertise could be made; I could discuss his use of a palette knife instead of a brush; I could talk about hue and saturation; I could say the sheer size, for the experience of walking into a room of these giants is similar to being cursed out volubly and violently, similar to being hit in the face by an object flying through the air at great speed.

*

For much of my late childhood and adolescence, I was afraid of expressing my opinion to others, fearing that if I did they might disagree with and so dislike me. Instead, I developed a reflexive habit of nearly always agreeing with others so that I would come across as agreeable and someone to like; I had a particularly nasty habit of not being able to admit when I was unaware of some reference being made and would find myself trapped in involved conversations about things about which I knew nothing, nodding my head furiously in agreement with the person with whom I was speaking.

Later, as a reaction against this tendency—which reached its apex when I was a freshman in high school and which apex led to much navel gazing, during which I began to see my inability to assert myself as evidence that I had an indistinct, weak personality—I took the opposite approach, by forcefully expressing my opinions and thoughts to others, regardless of whether or not an aggressive expression of one's opinion was really appropriate. In contrast to my formerly sheep-like self, I strove to become the sort of person whom others avoided disagreeing with. I wanted my stances known. I wanted to seem confident. Nobody was going to push me around. I was going to be an asshole.

As part of this project, I grew to admire assholes the world over, seeing in their force of personality a guide for my own behavior. It should come as little surprise that during this same period of time I was listening to a great deal of punk rock, the gist of much of which was giving the world the middle finger. In particular, when I was sixteen or so, I discovered the band Fugazi. Specifically, Fugazi's 1989 record *13 Songs*, as one is wont to do at sixteen. And more specifically, that record's first song, the anthemic post-hardcore classic "Waiting Room."

Nearly twenty years later, "Waiting Room" still kills me; if there was ever a song written to incite its listeners to throw clenched, fuck-yeah-that's-great fists in the air, then "Waiting Room" is that song. Aside from the music—with its heavy opening bassline and stuttered stops and starts and chorally yelled lines—the song's lyrics were precisely what I needed to hear at seventeen, as they reinforced loudly what I'd been telling myself for years: in the second verse, Fugazi's Ian MacKaye sings-screams *I won't sit idly by / I'm planning a big surprise / I'm gonna fight / for what I wanna be.* When I heard this, that afternoon after school in my high school's auditorium, where I was working on the set of an upcoming play as a member of the stage crew (something I'd gotten into several years earlier, mainly as an excuse to use dangerous tools with little adult supervision), I experienced a revelation. Even played through the beaten, dented little boom box that lived backstage, hearing "Waiting Room" that day changed my life. Thereafter, I was two selves: Kevin before "Waiting Room," and Kevin after. The latter version was a bit of a dick, I'm afraid.

*

And though such a sea change may sound like a bit of revisionist personal history, I really did change. I fought with my parents more. I cursed a lot (and still do). I drove faster. I dumped my nice, straightedge ska-loving girlfriend for a girl who drank and who had a somewhat more fun-loving reputation. And as an undergraduate—an undergraduate fine arts major, focused on installation and video, the very worst sort—I cultivated an interest in obscure art and music and the personality of the sort of person who enjoys obscure art and music at the expense of other more popular, broadly entertaining media: I worked on becoming a haughty dick who looked down his nose at people with more plebian interests, and took an especial interest in badmouthing the hippie "fraternity" on campus, who I felt were all a bunch of obnoxious trust fund brats driving their parents' older model Mercedes to and from the patchouli store.

It was roughly around this time that I began to admire Clyfford Still, and not just because I discovered his work in the midst of my interest-in-strange-art period. When I learned that Still was an asshole, the sort of "pure" artist who disdained public relations and commercial success in lieu of a fanatical devotion to his own work (and ego), I became so interested in him and his work that that interest bordered on obsession. Here was an artist I could emulate, I thought as I edited dissonant audio over grainy looping distortions of home movies in the pursuit of some sort of domestic commentary and meaning via video art; here was a guy I could model myself after. After all, famous dead artists are by nature mythical creatures. And famous dead artists who painted enormous inaccessible abstract paintings and seemingly hated the company of their fellow man are even more mythical and mysterious. Fuck everybody else, I want to be like Still, I thought.

*

However, age happens, and with age, the inevitable rounding of one's youth's sharp corners. Being an asshole unnecessarily, and going nearly everywhere in the world with a scowl on one's face, does not, I learned, get one far in the world. And being a dick is simply exhausting. Which is not to say I've reverted to my adolescent ways of agreeing with people about everything and pretending that I know about more cool shit than I really do (that still happens), but as with many things in life, a little moderation is what's called for.

In addition, I've come to realize what it is that really attracts me to Still's work. His paintings, despite their size and immense presence in a room, are works of extreme subtlety. Unlike some of his contemporaries—Pollock comes to mind, or Kandinsky—Still's work does not hit its viewers over the head with movement. And his color palette is basic—lots of primary colors and slightly dirtied primary colors. Moreover, Still's work does not resort to technical trickery and more radical, fourth-wall breaking techniques, like painting on strangely shaped canvases, or pulling a Rauschenberg and incorporating objects that sometimes hang from and so break up the borders of his works' frames. Rather, Still's work has a quiet, almost unassuming (or menacing, depending on one's perspective) presence, and it is this presence that one should really use as a model for one's behavior, far more than the model of one prickly cactus of an artist's dealings with other people. Though I've long disagreed with the New Critics, who would have us ignore artists' biographies in favor of an objective, context-free appraisal of their work, the New Critics did have a point. If an artist or writer is more famous for their poor behavior than their work, what does that say about their work? Luckily for Still, and for my love of his art, Still's work lives on not because he came across as "an avenging Protestant minister coming out of the barren lands of the Dakotas," but because, as Still himself said, his paintings *carry their own fire.*

The Other Woman

In the painting, she is the only other woman in the room. Like the female patient, as well as the clinicians operating on that patient, she is also wearing white, though the white she wears is only that of her high crenellated cap and of the apron she wears over her black clothes. The merest glimpse of her left hand lets you know she is holding something, a tray perhaps, that she has always been in the room holding a tray, that she is comfortable being the person in rooms of blood not engaged with that blood but instead being the person holding the tray and waiting to be called on by the men whose shirtsleeves have been rolled under their surgical gowns. Her eyes are heavy and ringed with red; she looks tired.

*

Dr. Agnew's mustache frames his face like a frown, and he furrows his brow as he gestures with his right hand and holds the scalpel, its tip pointing at the floor, quiescent, in his left hand, as he finishes making his point. We seem to have caught him midsentence, and his right hand, the hand whose fingers he is cupping upward in a sort of ball, is a visual piece of punctuation while he gathers his thoughts and moves on to the next point about mastectomy's mysteries while junior doctors apply chloroform and clear away blood and make an incision along the outside of the patient's left breast.

*

Commissioned in 1889 by a group of medical students, Thomas Eakins's *The Agnew Clinic* is his largest painting, measuring roughly seven feet by ten feet. It is heavily weighted to the right, as the painting's main action takes place in its lower right hand corner, where an operation is being performed on a female patient who is nude from the waist up; the patient's right breast is fully visible. This caused a stir at the time of the painting's execution. The doctor for whom the painting is named, David Hayes Agnew, is an unmistakable vision in white: he is gowned in white, his mustache and hair are white, and the top of his head—bald under his thinning hair—shines, seemingly reflecting a light being pointed at the operation. Dr. Agnew stands (from the viewer's perspective) to the left of the operation, by the partition wall separating the operating floor of the surgical theater from the men in attendance, who are nearly all dressed in dark suits. Many have their hair parted in the middle, many have beards, and at least two are wearing glasses. One, on the second tier behind Dr. Agnew, may be asleep, as he is bored by the entertainment—an entertainment in the form of surgery, to be precise—before him. Two others seem to be rather intimate, with one leaning his head on the other's shoulder while the other in turn leans the right side of his head against the top of his partner's head. An odd place and time for affection, or a trick of the light and perspective?

Thomas Eakins—who in 1875 had previously painted another surgical theater scene, his famous *The Gross Clinic* or *The Clinic of Dr. Gross*—was paid $750 by a group of Dr. Agnew's students from the University of Pennsylvania to paint this stunning, vivid painting in tones of oak and white and black and flesh and the steely glint of the scalpel in Dr. Agnew's hand. There are thirty-three faces visible in the painting, plus the lower halves of five or six additional bodies seated on the top row of the surgical theater's seats. Including Agnew, four physicians are performing a partial mastectomy on a woman lying on an operating table that is situated near the bottom-right-hand corner of the composition, over which a nurse stands still as stone, her glance cast somewhat down toward the patient whose upper half is uncovered and nude, but no, the patient doesn't mind, she has been sufficiently chloroformed to be nude in a room of probing male eyes, to be nude and operated upon in a room suffused with the male gaze.

As the British art critic John Berger noted, "Men look at women. Women watch themselves being looked at."

*

The nurse's manner is one of indifference, indifference to all of the gazing directed at the only other member of her sex in the room, indifference to blood and the smell of sweat coming off of the young resident stooped in front of her holding down the patient's right arm, and especially indifference to Agnew's bloviating, which she has no doubt heard before and which has become the white noise of her professional life. It is a swaggering, rolling incantation of observation and discovery that she has heard so often that it has become a sort of white noise, rather than the revelatory deliverances from a god, as Agnew intends it. His confidence, bordering on arrogance and smugness, is obvious from his body language: the casual way he leans against the theater's partition wall; the cocksure expression on his face; the way he brings his right shoulder up as he raises his hand to make a point on which he knows the men in dark suits will hang, on every syllable and word; and from his presence as the sole truly older man in the room, the only one with white hair in a chamber of the talented young and the curious middle-aged, he is a sort of god to them, insofar as all of our elders are minor gods, the fact that they've gone ahead of us in life gifting them knowledge and experiences that we can only attain by continuing to wait. *Pfffff* thinks the nurse dismissively. *Just listen to him go on.*

*

From David Hayes Agnew's *The Principles and Practice of Surgery*, 1889:

Women possessing a very excitable nervous system, with hysterical tendencies, are not favorable subjects for an operation, especially one of severity; and, when added to this organization there exists a feeble heart, the dangers are greatly increased. Such persons are incapable of withstanding the effects of shock, and often sink under the consequent exhaustion. Mere nervous excitement, if not associated with despondency, does not contra-indicate an operation. Persons of such a temperament, though they suffer much, both in body and in mind, soon recover their usual flow of spirits, which, acting like a cordial, serves to hasten recovery.

*

What does our nurse think as she stands there holding a tray, doing her best to ignore Agnew's latest observation? Does she think of the weight of the tray in her arms, the overpowering scents of men and cologne and stale cigar smoke and the remnants of cordial after lunch and chloroform and blood in the room? Does she think of the woman on the operating table, and how she and the patient aren't all that different, that what separates the two of them is only the merest fraction of fate? Maybe she thinks of the children she does not yet have. Or maybe she thinks of the disappointments and setbacks—even if she did start out the granddaughter of immigrants, living in a small town to the north still dominated by agriculture—that led to her standing in this room of men and blood, waiting on these foreign creatures they call *doctors*, these men who view life as a series of problems to be solved until the problems become so intractable only death can solve them. And then maybe she thinks of how Agnew—standing against the partition making another point while the tip of his scalpel glistens with the patient's blood—has experienced so few setbacks and/ or rejections, how only others' lives have been for him problems to solve while his life presented no difficulties whatsoever, a good birth leading to a good school leading to a good match and a wedding announcement and healthy children emerging as if scripted to do so, and throughout it all the sort of career one's grandchildren and great-grandchildren will boast about for years to come. Maybe she thinks about fairness, and jealousy.

*

Thomas Eakins knew his fair share of setbacks and rejections. To wit, from Sidney Kirkpatrick's 2006 book *The Revenge of Thomas Eakins*:

> ...although [Eakins] had once distinguished himself as an art student in Paris and traveled widely throughout Europe, he lived and worked virtually his entire career in the accommodating but modest Philadelphia rowhouse where he grew up. He married late in life, had no children, and spent his nonworking hours with friends and admirers, many of them students and fellow sportsmen. Had it not been for financial support from his doting father, he might well have given up painting altogether to pursue a career in medical science, a field that interested in nearly as much as art.

Eakins's troubles sprang, broadly, from his stubborn devotion to the absolutely realistic—without idealization, warts and all—way he depicted the world and the people that populate it. He was interested in photography; he painted male nudes and exposed students of both sexes to nude models of both sexes; he painted anatomical grotesqueries, like the surgery being performed in the aforementioned *The Gross Clinic*; he married one of his students when he was forty and still living in his father's house (with his father). Indeed, only three years before the commission of *The Agnew Clinic,* Eakins was forced to resign from his position as director of what is now the Pennsylvania Academy of the Fine Arts. And so on.

Such stories—of artists who have been forgotten or misunderstood and/or dismissed during their lifetimes—are unsurprising because they are so common. Herman Melville worked as a customs inspector. Marcel Proust died before most of *À la recherche du temps perdu* saw the light of day, and he was forced to self-publish its first volume because of editorial disinterest. Walt Whitman was a similarly self-made man, as he printed the earliest editions of *Leaves of Grass* himself, in between stints as a newspaperman, army nurse, Bureau of Indian Affairs clerk, and teacher. The poet Wallace Stevens was an insurance executive.

Since I began working at sixteen, I have been a stock boy at a grocery; have pumped gas; have organized the archives of the *American Poetry Review*; I have moved unwanted furniture and other detritus out of dorm rooms; have stood at a cash register for hours on end, and watched an endless line of customers curl around a bookstore; have recorded cigar and wine-related tasting notes; have made photocopies and designed sales spreadsheets and packed boxes and flown to book conventions where I shook hands and ate richly and at night took taxis drunkenly back to my hotel room; have read comic books when I should have been reviewing budgets and tinkering with presentations; have taught undergraduates how to write fiction when I can hardly do so myself; have, at twenty-eight, pushed a library cart and shelved books; have edited book proposals; have sat at the back of a large room full of pharmaceutical executives wearing suits and listened to a former FBI agent telling a story that involved a truckload of stolen antacids to warm up the crowd; and I have written about diseases and the poor sick people they invade, far too often.

Such a recitation of past employment fills me with both nostalgia (remember hiding in the freezer, gloved and jacketed, eating from the damaged carton of Rocky Road when I should have been stocking vegetables?) and fear, as it does not yet, nor will it likely ever, include "making the art that I want to make, as my job." For what is success but the recognition that you do what you're doing well enough for the world to continue to allow you to do it? Not that I haven't become inured to rejections and setbacks. I have. But being rejected by even the smallest journal or press—possessing a small to nonexistent readership in a landscape glutted with similarly tiny literary journals and presses—makes me worry that my grand hope of attempting to make art is doomed, and that any work I do produce (like this very sentence) is destined not for some audience (however miniscule) but the void. Who, if anyone, will read all of these words?

*

According to the National Assessment of Adult Literacy, from the National Center for Education Statistics, in 1890, only one year after Eakins painted *The Agnew Clinic*, overall illiteracy among adults in the U.S. stood at 13.3 percent (as of 1979 it was 0.6 percent). In 1890, 56.8 percent of blacks couldn't read, nor could 13.1 percent of foreign-born whites. Another report, from the U.S. Commissioner of Education, notes that between 1889 and 1890 23.18 percent of the U.S. population was enrolled in some sort of school (elementary on up), while 0.58 percent was enrolled in secondary instruction and a mere 0.22 percent was enrolled in "superior" or college instruction. Now for some fuzzy math. Based on the 1890 census's account of the overall U.S. population, which comes to 62,622,250, this means that just under 140,000 students (most of whom were no doubt men) were enrolled in U.S. colleges. Moreover, according to the NIH, in 1900 there were 25,000 medical students and 5,200 graduates enrolled in medical schools across the U.S. So that's 30,200 medical students total (i.e., .04 percent of the population in 1900) divided by the 45 states of the Union in 1900 = 671 medical students per state, on average (though this is certainly inaccurate; most students were studying on the Eastern Seaboard).

The point being that men like Agnew and the dark-suited cronies that surround him in *The Agnew Clinic* were rare specimens indeed, the most privileged of the privileged class, possessing knowledge that few of their peers, and indeed few in the world, possessed. And yet among mere mortals they were forced to walk every day, indeed even being forced to interact with them from time to time. Including frequently those mortals known as nurses who, though they were educated after a fashion—at the time, nurses had to pass through several years of training, mainly in the clinic and not the classroom, and all could certainly read—were hardly schooled to the degree Dr. Agnew, his colleagues, and the students who commissioned Eakins (who himself was highly educated, albeit artistically: before he taught there, he attended the Pennsylvania Academy, then studied anatomy, then studied painting in France for four years) to paint *The Agnew Clinic* were. The nurse who stands sentinel in the painting may well be the only member of the middle or lower classes in the painting. And she is a sign that the world is changing, a sign that not only will members of the less privileged classes be initiated into the mysteries of ether and suture, but that they will also be women. And that they will not remain nameless.

*

Her name was Mary V. Clymer, or Mary U. Clymer, depending on one's source, and she was "a native of upstate Pennsylvania," who had come to Philadelphia to attend nursing school, according to a brief history by University of Pennsylvania nursing historian Joan Lynaugh. Clymer kept a diary and lecture notes, in which she recorded things like the following:

> Thursday. On duty at seven. From seven to nine served food. Gave after-food medicines. Temperatures, sweeping, and cleaning gone through and finished. The typhoid still

worse. Put away the clean linen. Sponged the three ty-
phoid cases and bathed them with alcohol. Cut bread and
made preparations for dinner. Off to dinner and back at
12 noon. Busy until 2 PM. Off until four, changed a paralyzed patient—have learned to do it without assistance.

*

Though *The Agnew Clinic's* stated subject is David Hayes Agnew, the
viewer's eye is not pulled toward Dr. Agnew but toward the surgical
procedure on the painting's right, over which Nurse Clymer looms
like a muffled exclamation mark. Try as one might, one cannot help
being pulled from Dr. Agnew's gesturing figure back toward his assistants huddled around the unconscious patient and Nurse Clymer's
heavily lidded eyes pointing neither down at the procedure before
her nor out at the viewers. And even when one does manage to keep
one's gaze directed at Dr. Agnew—to, for a moment, examine what
seem to be spots of blood hidden among the folds of his gown—she
is always there, at the edge of one's vision, the peak of her cap reminiscent of the points crowning the Statue of Liberty's head, which
was completed only three years prior to Eakins's commission. While
Agnew's manner may be arrogant and smug, she possesses a different
sort of self-assurance, an assurance borne out of being steadfast and
self-made. Her steady presence in the room, unwavering even in the
face of violence enacted in the name of medical progress and the great
fight against death, shows us an alternative to Agnew's method of
being remembered. Some boast and bluster, while others simply are.
Patience, counsels Nurse Clymer under her breath, as Dr. Agnew's
assistants bustle before her. *Patience*, she whispers across the centuries,
patience is a virtue.

That Knot in Your Stomach

Phlegm / Blood / Yellow Bile / Black Bile

The Ancient Greeks, followed by the Romans and Persians, followed by a procession of European physicians, philosophers, quacks, and writers, believed that the human body was regulated by interactions among the four "humours," which were phlegm, blood, yellow bile, and black bile. When these elements were in harmony, so was the body. When they fell out of harmony, so did one's health.

Which includes one's mental disposition. The Ancient Greek physician Hippocrates, as translated by Charles Darwin Adams, noted that "as long as the brain is at rest, the man enjoys his reason, but the depravement of the brain arises from phlegm and bile…" Those made mad by phlegm, Hippocrates said, are quiet, while those mad from some imbalance of bile "are vociferous, malignant, and will not be quiet, but are always doing something improper."

According to the logic of the humours, one's mental and physical wellbeing, or lack thereof, originated from the same sources. Treat an imbalance of black bile—the Greek word for which was *melas/melanos* (black) + *khole* (bile), which leads one to the Greek *melankhola* (sadness) and our *melancholy*—that is causing a patient's gastrointestinal distress, and you might also end up curing their bad mood. Which is a much more convenient explanation for melancholy and depression than the thousand natural shocks, per Hamlet, that we endure from the rising to the setting of the sun. And maybe, just maybe, the idea, however discredited by hundreds of years of medical progress, that physical and mental diseases arise in the same place, might help to explain why my mother developed and was eventually killed by cancer.

Albrecht Dürer's 1514 engraving *Melencolia I* depicts a melancholic winged female angel figure sitting before a tower festooned with symbols (a bell, a panel of strange letters, an hourglass, a scale) with her head resting on her left hand as she holds a long metal compass in her lap, and she is looking up and to her right at the title of the piece, *Melencolia I,* a graphic of which is flying from the horizon and seems to be held by some sort of bat.

It's an immensely busy image: in addition to the aforementioned imagery, the engraving also contains a sleeping dog, a cherub reading, various tools, what looks like a half-carved block of granite, and off in the distance a city on the water, among other things. The Swiss art historian Heinrich Wölfflin wrote that the picture contains "a chaos of objects." And for his part, the Polish art historian Wojciech Balus said *Melencolia I* and the objects it contains and what those objects might *mean*—all of which have been the object of great academy attention—amount to "frequently enumerated ambiguities."

At the time Dürer produced Melencolia I melancholy was closely associated with genius (this notion persists today). Aristotle, writing long before Dürer, wondered in his *Problems* why "is it that all men who have become outstanding in philosophy, statesmanship, poetry or the arts are melancholic, and some to such an extent that they are infected by the diseases arising from black bile..." So Dürer's engraving is a depiction of sadness and melancholy as the medium for inspiration; inspiration and depression are inextricably linked.

But it's not as if being depressed is desirable, given that depression often equals feeling like hell and finding little pleasure in the act of being alive, even if depression might also equal inspiration. But let's say there is a connection between melancholic moods and the artistic temperament; after all, there is evidence thereof in the scientific literature. For example, a 2011 *British Journal of Psychiatry* paper pointed out a "familial cosegregation of both schizophrenia and bipolar disorder with creativity is suggested." Even so, it's not as if depressed persons would necessarily choose to stay depressed if remaining miserable meant they painted better or wrote more insightfully, for depression is miserable. Would one rather mimic a depressed but artistically successful but ultimately self-destructive artist (examples of which are legion), or some kindly octogenarian retired taxi driver of a grandfather, who during his days knew mostly dull work but also sometimes laughter and the odd trip to the Ozarks and who, when he did die, did so surrounded by family and grandchildren too bubbly for such a solemn occasion?

Then again, another study published in *Psychiatria Danubina* points out that "[n]ot all writers and artists suffer from major mood disorders. Likewise, most people who have a major mood disorder are not writers or artists." Casting aside this debate, let us return to the art historians. Melancholy, says Balus of *Melencolia I*, is:

> a state of undecidability. The state occurs as a mental disease, imprisoning the afflicted man in a circle of matters insolvable for him, or as a passing indisposition brought about by his character or spiritual mood. In all cases its effect is invariably the same—depression accompanied by fear, an inner state akin to silence, and a highly specific perception of the world as undergoing diffusion, a process of losing sense.

Which state, of a person gradually "losing sense," largely describes my mother's mood from roughly the fall of 1998 until her cancer diagnosis in the spring of 2008. When my father killed himself in October 1998 he didn't just kill himself: he killed my mother too, though it took more than a decade for her to die. She was never the same after his death. Though my mother was always a stern figure—I have many memories of my hair being roughly combed early in the morning before school, against my will—what *joie de vivre* she possessed before my father's wholly unexpected suicide was muffled by his death. The opening lines of "Dream Song 29" by the poet John Berryman[11]—in which a "thing ... só heavy" sits down on the poem's subject's heart, that even if the poem's subject had a hundred years, even that would not be enough time to heal the wound—is an apt summation of the hurt my father's suicide caused my mother. His death was the heavy thing that sat down on my mother's heart, and try as she might, she could not make good again. Which is not to say that the years between his death and hers were wholly grim, nor were they a waste. The things happy people do she continued to do, albeit sporadically. She laughed; she played the Beatles and Bonnie Raitt on the CD player in our kitchen; she got drunk at a wedding and danced; she briefly dated a man who was in the middle of a divorce; she stuck to the routine of work and domesticity and helped put me and my sisters through college; she put up with my listless progress into adulthood; and she tolerated my scotch-induced blubbering at Sam's wedding, next to the dessert buffet.

Nonetheless, after my father's death there was some part of my mother that was missing and which no one, not her children, not her sisters, not her therapist—who eventually became less of her therapist and more her friend, so often did my mother visit her—could put back together again. Her melancholy was not that of *Melencolia I,* the sort of malaise that also inspires; her melancholy was the type no one sings about and of which no engravings are made. Cold, meager meals in cold rooms, recriminations on the phone, and a growing bitterness in one's insides. All the king's horses and all the king's men.

---

11   Who was himself a depressed alcoholic whose father killed himself and who himself later committed suicide by jumping from the Washington Avenue Bridge in Minneapolis

But But But But But But

Surely then there must be some link—aside from that espoused by the ancients—between one's mental state and the health burdens one carries, surely? Surely my mother's cancer was to some extent caused by the black seed in her gut, planted by my father's death and nurtured by the anger and melancholy she suffered in the years following his death? Surely, raising five children by herself, not to mention suffering through the minor jabs of work and childrearing and commuting and the fluorescent glow of supermarket lighting, got to be too much after a while, surely? Surely there are causes and effects in this world that, though they may be invisible at the time of their occurrence, are able to be seen as clear as a magnetic resonance imaging printout held up in front of the stricken patient's face in an examination room where the only sounds are the whisper of air from a vent and the creaking crackle of one's bottom shifting uncomfortably on the thin white paper covering the examination table?

Unsurprisingly, the jury that is scientific consensus on this issue remains out. To wit, some "findings suggest that the overall effect size for a causal association between personality and cancer is extremely small," noted Naoki Nakaya, in the *Journal of Epidemiology*. Meaning there's probably not a connection between one's mental state and whether or not one develops advanced inoperable metastatic colorectal cancer in one's fifties despite a lifetime of healthy eating and exercise, for example. And furthermore: A study published in the *British Journal of Cancer*, in which a group of Dutch researchers examined more than 8000 subjects, more than 1000 of whom experienced "self-reported stressful major life events," found no association with increased cancer risk.

However, somewhat contradicting the above studies is a *Journal of the National Cancer Institute* investigation of cancer incidence in post-Holocaust European Jews. This one found "statistically significantly higher rates for all-site, breast, and colorectal cancers" among those study participants exposed to the Holocaust as opposed to

Europeans Jews who fled Europe for Israel before World War II broke out. The authors posit a number of reasons prolonged stress (both physical as well as mental) may well have led to cancer—perhaps, they note, stress leads to cancer-causing activities, like smoking—but the overall point is that they found an association between experiencing extreme stress and higher incidence of cancer. Indeed, the authors of that study's accompanying editorial, "Cancer Risk From Extreme Stressors: Lessons From European Jewish Survivors of World War II," wrote that:

> …data from animal and human studies indicate that although calorie restriction is typically associated with decreased cancer risk, the anticancer effects of calorie restriction may be neutralized or overwhelmed by extreme stressors.

Calorie restriction aside—one sees many very thin cancer researchers at conferences—the upshot of this study is: So you're saying there's a chance sadness and cancer could be connected? Then again, it's not as if the mind-boggling "stress" (*stress* being far too banal a word) that Holocaust survivors experienced is in any way similar to the sorts of stresses experienced by middle-class white Americans, so studies like the above aren't particularly applicable to patients outside of those who have come through a version of hell on earth and survived. More common are the daily tragedies we face in some form or another: the loss of a loved one; a malignant diagnosis; or the myriad financial, professional, or personal setbacks that prick like pins throughout one's days. And, of course, feeling low.

So yes, maybe there is a there there, when it comes to depression and cancer. Though the link between psychological stressors like depression and cancer is "elusive," notes Michael R. Irwin in the *Journal of Clinical Oncology*, another 1998 *Journal of the National Cancer Institute* study, led by Brenda Penninx, found an association between cancer risk and long-term depression in the elderly. An 88 percent increased risk in fact, in chronically depressed persons 71 years and older. "The excess risk of cancer associated with chronically depressed mood was consistent for most types of cancer and was not limited to cigarette smokers," Penninx et al. write.

Of course my mother wasn't elderly when she was diagnosed; she was middle-aged and had recently gone through menopause. Her hair wasn't fully gray yet. She exercised. She drove cautiously and went on long walks. She doted on the pets. She flew to Minneapolis to see me, and I made her the vodka sauce recipe I like to make wherein one soaks red pepper flakes in the vodka *before* adding both to an already simmering sauce.

Maybe, then, there isn't necessarily a connection between her mood—during her visit to Minneapolis she was lonely and sad, and talked to me about her sadness, which was disconcerting—and the cancer diagnosis that would spring upon her fewer than six months later. Maybe by searching for answers like this, one is less hoping to find a satisfying answer than to immerse oneself in the search, and by being so immersed forget the original pain that led one to conduct such a search in the first place, forgetting what it was one was searching for in the first place when getting sidetracked by lists of compound German words (e.g., *quasselstrippe,* "motormouth") and essays about Camus written by spiritually tortured anesthesiologists.

A Purging, a Cleansing

Our word *catharsis* comes almost unchanged from the Ancient Greek: the adjective καθαρος (katharos), physically clean; spotless, and the participle καθαρσις (katharsis), cleansing from guilt or clearing of morbid humours, led to the Latin version of the word, *catharmos,* purification rites, and thence to our sense of a purging of tension, of a release that brings with it relief, an understanding that functions as an ending, a peaceful spiritual acceptance.

However, I've begun to suspect that catharsis might be too much to ask for. And that asking for catharsis is doomed from the start, because in seeking catharsis one is seeking an end that allows one to move on with the rest one's life. And this is foolish because things never really end, but instead continue and experiences merge into other experiences that merge into memories that jumble over each other like eager young children chasing a soccer ball on a foggy morning in October, all crowded chaotically around the object of their affection, the air fuzzy with their breath's fog.

Rather, I prefer to borrow from the literary theorist Kenneth Burke. In his essay "Literature as Equipment for Living," Burke points out that works of art "could be considered as designed to organize and command the army of one's thoughts and images, and to so organize them that" one "seeks to direct the larger movements and operations in one's campaign of living." Expanding on this, how should I "organize and command the army" of my thoughts to better confront, and engage with, the world? Maybe discursive essays. Maybe etymology. Maybe long walks around lakes at dusk in the summer when there are few bugs and a breeze drifts in from the west like a lover's breath.

"Even though I feel the qualitative absurdity of my quantifiable experiences, I continue to struggle with what is meaningful and doable," wrote the aforementioned spiritually tortured anesthesiologist Thomas Jon Papadimos in a commentary published in *The Permanente Journal* on Camus's "The Myth of Sisyphus" vis-à-vis Papadimos's daily experience as a critical care physician. Camus's essay, about his concept of the absurd, notes Dr. Papadimos, conflicts with Papadimos's daily life as someone who fights the good fight against death, when he knows many of his patients will die, even if they don't know it themselves.[12] And you know what, Papadimos more or less writes, the contradiction between the two—Camus's absurdism and

---

12   In short, the certainty of eventual death, in a God-free universe that is unreasonable and uncaring, renders all of our activity absurd, particularly the human desire to find meaning.

Papadimos's need to grapple with the world—is kind of a bummer. Nonetheless, the essay ends on an affirmation: "I am not impaired or paralyzed by the thunderous silence of the cosmos."

Nor, it seems, was my mother after her cancer diagnosis. Though I have occasionally felt that the cosmos pulses and roars with malice, offering little in the way of catharsis or tactical strategies, after my mom received her news—which was undeniably terrible, as stories involving stage four metastatic colorectal cancer tend not to end well—she seemed buoyed, almost happy even. Oddly, the lonesome knot of sadness and rage and bitterness in her stomach, which birthed an even bigger, truly Gordian knot of rapidly multiplying cancer cells that spread to her liver and beyond, seemed to be what unwound the original knot and allowed her to thrive during those last months. It was as if the diagnosis gave her something to live for. Or more appropriately for her personality[13] the cancer gave her an object on which to fix her attention, into which object's teeth she could throw her defiance. As if, for that last year or so, she were the winged figure in *Melencolia I* come to life, only she was no longer gazing into the distance with a look of demure thoughtfulness in her eyes, but was instead staring directly at the engraving's viewer (and the cancer, and the capricious world that had dished it out) with a smirk on her face and a challenge in her eyes, as if she were saying *come on, come on, fuck you, cancer.*

---

13   As my uncle said at her funeral, "Frannie had an edge."

Umbrellas

We found it funnier than we should have that our coworker Becca called Duane Reade—properly pronounced "Dwayne Read"—the nonsensical "Doo-wan Rea-dy." Because she'd lived in New York as the rest of us transplants, her mispronunciation of New York's signature drug store, a store at which New Yorkers seemed to shop nearly constantly, using Duane Reades the way one imagines people in prairie towns of yore used general stores, was incomprehensible. How could one screw up its name?

During my time in New York, Duane Reades—and drugstores in general—served more than any other kind of establishment as neighborhood landmarks, as anchors that helped me to situate myself in Manhattan. I spent an inordinate amount of time and money in a succession of Duane Reades, mostly at those near my various workplaces, using them as pharmacies as well as grocery stores, places in which to kill time, and particularly as repositories of cheap umbrellas. I bought, and discarded once they'd been broken by wind tearing through the skyscrapers' canyons, *a lot* of cheap umbrellas. My experience of living in New York was marked by the succession of budget umbrellas I always seemed to be purchasing or needing to purchase. After all, no one wants to be caught out in the rain; no one wants to make their arrival sodden and dripping, having attempted to run between the raindrops and then sitting in a puddle of one's own on the subway, water dripping down into one's eyes.

*

2005: the year of the rooster. It was a year of distant conflict; of terrorism and the threat of terrorism; heavily armed members of the military peering into subway cars, their guns long and black; a year I began to suspect that I was turning into an underachiever but didn't have the energy to do anything about it, and instead went to parties; the year of Hurricane Katrina; and the year the British pop group Broadcast's album *Tender Buttons* (named after the 1914 Gertrude Stein book) was released. *Tender Buttons* the record is, like its literary namesake, an odd bird. Technically electronic pop, the music on *Tender Buttons* is minimal and should not be fun, but it often is, though more in a bopping-one's-head-alone way rather than club fare.

Take, for example, "Michael A. Grammar," a "sawtooth wave" of a song addressed to a subject whose "father was a Teddy Boy"[14] in which the name Michael (which is sung Mi-chael, — ∪) is repeated so much that the name's trochee dominates the song. For example:

> Michael
> Michael Michael
> I'll change my hair but inside I'll stay the same
> Michael
> Michael Michael
> I'll draw my lips around my lipstick

The song, and much of the album as a whole, is infectious and fun but also a bit morose. This is largely because of Broadcast's lead singer Trish Keegan's intimate voice; when she sings it seems as if she is singing solely for you, and not for anyone else who might be in earshot. So on "Michael A. Grammar" when she sings "My feet are dancing so much / And I hate that my feet are dancing so much," I—who listened to *Tender Buttons* more or less continuously on the subway— felt that she was singing directly to me. You're right, I thought, I have been dancing too much, I have been playing when I should have been working, falling asleep on the train and closing bars, stumbling home at five in the morning into an apartment I can't afford, not making

---

14   A briefly popular and sometimes violent British 50s subculture of mostly young men who dressed like Edwardians, hence "Teddy"

art or writing or even thinking about doing either. I hate that, I do, I do, I hate it.

2005 was also the year I finally saw Christo's art in person. Or rather, a piece by Christo and Jeanne-Claude, as the Bulgarian and French-born, respectively, husband-and-wife duo branded themselves after 1994 (previously, Jeanne-Claude had been the silent partner). Initially famous for their wrapped pieces—in which the artists would wrap objects or buildings in fabric, like the Pont Neuf or the Reichstag—they also produced large-scale temporary environmental installations. The 2005 work in question was *The Gates*, the last project the couple would realize before Jeanne-Claude's death in 2009. And though the work—which comprises 7,503 sixteen-foot-high orange (or saffron, as Christo and Jeanne-Claude's description of the project insists) steel gates with orange fabric panels hanging from each gate, strewn across 23 miles of Central Park's walkways—underwhelmed, that I was finally seeing Christo's work in person was itself significant.

As an undergraduate I'd seen the 1978 film *Running Fence*, about the 1976 project in which Christo and an army of assistants stretched an eighteen-foot-high "fence" of white fabric 24.5 miles across Sonoma and Marin counties in California. The fence ran west, from just north of Petaluma to just south of Bodega Bay, where it terminated in the Pacific Ocean, and I found the film's shots of the fence's fabric rippling in a light breeze, running into the horizon and bifurcating the goldenrod-yellow, dry California hills on which it was installed, to be deeply stirring. *Running Fence* may be the one thing most responsible for the several years I spent fantasizing about the glamorous lives of installation artists (little did I know). Seeing *The Gates* then—at a point in my life when my poorly conceived dreams of ending up like Allan Kaprow (performance art pioneer) or Anne Hamilton (installation artist) had faded into long days doing work I was barely interested in, to pay the bills I'd somehow become responsible for—was exciting, and felt like it should have been significant. Maybe this, I told myself, is the shot in the arm I need to start making art again, to start being serious again. It was also exciting because of the aura of danger involved: what if one of those many sixteen-foot-high orange steel constructions were to fall on and crush me?

After all it wouldn't be the first time, as Christo and Jeanne-Claude's art had killed before. Twice in fact, during the showing and removal of their 1984-1991 cross-Pacific Ocean project, *The Umbrellas*. On October 26, 1991, one of the 3,100 nineteen-and-a-half-feet-high, 485-pound aluminum, fabric, steel, and wood umbrellas the artists had installed in California and Japan was picked up by high winds, "crushing a 33-year-old Camarillo, Calif., woman, Lori Mae Matthew, against a boulder," per *The New York Times*. Then on October 31, Masaaki Nakamuri was killed when the crane he was using to remove one of blue umbrellas installed in Japan (California got yellow, Japan blue) touched a high-voltage wire.

If Christo and Jeanne-Claude's appropriated version of umbrellas could kill, I wondered as I walked around Central Park the bright crisp Saturday morning we'd chosen for our visit to *The Gates*, wouldn't gates be as much if not more of a threat? After all, gates carry all of the usual associations with death and passing into the afterlife, but umbrellas? Save for the superstitious prohibition against leaving them open indoors, umbrellas are protective, beneficial tools, carrying goodwill. Umbrellas are designed to protect, against all sorts of things, from rain, to hail, to sun. And, as I would later learn, blood clots.

*

After my mother had her first stroke—an unfortunate side effect of the bevacuzimab she'd been given to treat her cancer—her doctors decided it would be prudent for her to get an umbrella installed. Properly known as an inferior vena cava filter, an "umbrella" filter offers a line of defense against deep vein thrombosis, a blood clot that has formed in a deep vein and which can cause a pulmonary embolism should it travel to the lungs. Inserted into the inferior vena cava (IVC), the large vein that carries deoxygenated blood from the heart, many IVC filters look like umbrella ribs, with the ribs pointing down; imagine that you are carrying an umbrella and are caught in a stiff wind, and that your umbrella is turned inside-out. This is more or less what many IVC filters look like, without an umbrella's fabric. One particular brand of IVC filter, the "Simon Nitinol Vena Cava Filter," manufactured by Bard Peripheral Vascular, even has an umbrella-esque assemblage of wires above the down-pointing, hook-ended ribs. Per a *Blood* paper on IVC filter types and use, "at body temperature, the wires are programmed to unfold into an umbrella filter composed of 7 'petals' and 6 hooked legs that anchor the device in the vena cava."

Despite carrying the umbrella name, many IVC filters don't really look like umbrellas. At least not when compared to the now-outdated, original IVC umbrella filter, the Mobin-Uddin Umbrella, invented by the late Kazi Mobin-Uddin, MD, who created his device in the late 1960s. Unlike later iterations of IVC filters, Dr. Mobin-Uddin's filter—which is round and looks like an umbrella seen from above, albeit one whose protective fabric has been pierced through—was a solid honeycombed with holes that "allowed the blood to flow through the perforations but trapped clots that would otherwise travel to lungs," per a *Journal of the Islamic Medical Association of North America* paper. "Simply put the umbrella allowed the rain to go through but stopped the hail."

And though there were modifications and improvements on the original, it seems the "umbrella" name stuck. In part, I suspect, because of the protective connotations umbrellas carry, and likewise because the negative, calamitous connotations rain carries (especially being caught out in the rain, in a sudden storm far too plentiful for crops and sewers, causing rivers to overrun their banks and bridge pilings to loosen, the apocalyptic Flood we fear in our bones) is an appropriate metaphor for sudden stroke and embolism-causing thromboses.

*

But of course we cannot hold back the flood. "Maybe," said a Japanese woman featured in the Maysles' film *Umbrellas*, of the deaths caused by Christo and Jeanne-Claude's umbrella project, "it was because he added something artificial to nature." Try as they might, the artists' years of planning and meticulous umbrella design couldn't withstand the winds whipping through California's Tejon Pass, nor could they protect against our tendency toward daydream and/or error, even in the face of low-hanging power lines.

"Whenever you add something artificial to nature ... there are consequences," the woman *in Umbrellas* continued. "We don't know the power of nature. Even though the structure was strong enough to withstand the severity of nature, nature has unimaginable power."

Likewise, maybe it was the removal of my mother's medication that led to her conclusive strokes, or maybe it was that the umbrella filter's delicate structure was too weak. I imagine now that her doctors thought the combination of the anticoagulants she was already receiving, plus the umbrella filter, would protect her against future strokes. And they were right, for a while, until her treatment failed and she went into hospice and was taken off of all her medications, after which point she proceeded to have a number of what I am pretty sure were ischemic strokes, before the inevitable, interminable end. Maybe there was nothing we could do, or maybe we didn't do enough. Maybe we won't run out of time. Maybe we won't get caught in the rain again. Maybe we should have thought to buy a new umbrella, for our old ones are a sorry mess. But maybe, maybe, maybe it won't rain, even though the sky has begun to gray ominously and the trees' leaves are turning themselves over in expectation.

Ports and Dockings

Plastic: *'plas-tik: from the Latin* plasticus*: "capable of shaping or molding": having a quality suggestive of mass-produced goods: artificial.*

In April 2008, when my mother called to tell me that the flu that had laid her up for weeks wasn't in fact the flu but was in fact stage-four colon cancer, I prepared myself for a number of things. Because her cancer was so advanced, she'd be receiving chemotherapy immediately, which would make her lose her hair. After all that's what people with advanced inoperable cancers did, they went on chemo and lost their hair: okay. And okay, she'd probably lose weight and look very thin the next time I flew home from Minnesota; she did have advanced inoperable cancer. She'd be weak; she'd get tired easily; her eyes would be bloodshot; her skin would be paler than usual; and her fingers would probably be somehow seemingly longer and bonier than they were pre-cancer: all things I'd seen in other sick people.

But her port? I wasn't prepared for her port.

A *port* is what it sounds like: an opening in which something— in my mother's case an IV— can dock. People build ports for ships because doing so makes more sense than having boats pull up at random to shores; without ports every time ships made land they'd have to negotiate shifting sandbars and deal with the difficulty of launching boats across the shallows; ports, convenient and efficient, eliminate this hassle. Likewise for the human body, and medicine. A medical port—a *Port-a-Cath* or *Microport* or *Medi-port,* depending on the brand—is a semi-permanent catheterized injection bullseye installed beneath (though bulging slightly up from) the skin, designed to make the repeated delivery of drugs to a patient that much easier. Why bother trying to find a vein every time a chronically ill patient comes in for treatment when you can simply stick a needle into that patient's port?

But, of course, the difference is that one builds a port meant for ships *onto* a shoreline, whereas a medical port is inserted *into* a person, and that (of course) building ports in the earth is a very different matter from inserting plastic nozzles and tubes into people. Onto, into, into, onto. My mother's port, which was flesh-tan and plastic, was inserted under the skin above her clavicle, on her right side, its roundness protruding obscenely. My mother's port bumped the skin under which it rested up about half an inch; beneath her skin the port was connected to what was probably my mother's subclavian vein by a long, tubular, white catheter. Were it removed from her body and laid on its side, the port would resemble a single gigantic sperm: big head, long winding tail after. My mother's port's obtrusion seemed to suggest that she wasn't all flesh and bones, nor were any of us and that, in fact, strange plastic parts could sometimes be found beneath anyone's skin.

I only saw her port a handful of times, the first and most significant of which was the time I accompanied her to the clinic so that she could receive chemotherapy. Rather than forcing all of their cancer patients to go to a general hospital for treatment, my mother's health system had set up a handful of cancer-specific clinics, like cancer-only satellites. This was smart but depressing, the kind of cold, accountant's logic which seems to too often dominate health systems: because of the clinic's specificity every patient there had cancer. See that man over there? Cancer. Her, the mother of two who seems so young? Cancer. And so on; the clinic's very existence was evidence of how pervasive cancer, or at least the treatment of cancer, has seemingly become, that there are now so many people with so many forms of cancer (200 and counting!) that it makes sense to set those with cancer aside. Moreover, the range of people receiving treatment disturbed me deeply: this was not a place only for the old and the feeble, but one for everyone; cancer is, if nothing else, a democratic disease. While waiting I could too easily visualize myself visiting such a clinic at some point in the future, when I myself had cancer.

Finally it was my mother's turn, so to the back of the clinic we went. I assumed my mother would be given her own tiny room, but no such luck: we were shuttled into a sort of hallway. This hallway was partitioned into a number of sections like open cubicles, and in each section was a large medical chair, in which the patient would sit while receiving treatment; each chair was surrounded by instruments and monitors, by all of the technological effluvia of healing. More importantly, there were snacks. Lining the cubicle-hallway were a number of fridges filled with sodas and bins of crackers and the like, of which both the patient as well as the patient's family were encouraged to avail themselves. So while I greedily ate my pretzels and drank my Coke, my mother's nurse arrived to insert her IV. To do so, she slipped the hem of my mother's shirt down a bit, and there *it* was: her port.

*

An aside, *sotto voce*: from the 1967 film *The Graduate*:

> **Mr. McGuire:** I want to say one word to you. Just one word.
>
> **Benjamin:** Yes, sir.
>
> **Mr. McGuire:** Are you listening?
>
> **Benjamin:** Yes I am.
> **Mr. McGuire:** Plastics.
>
> **Benjamin:** Exactly how do you mean?

*

How indeed? Though artificial, plastics are benign, or at least their history began benignly (and so we must believe, for they're too omnipresent for us to not believe them to be harmless): plastics were invented to replace products that the natural world had previously supplied (and the supply of which people were rapidly running through). To wit, celluloid was originally invented to replace ivory, and in particular ivory billiards balls; rayon was inspired by silkworms; nylon replaced animal hair; Velcro was modeled after cockleburs.

Okay, but where does it all come from? In short, oil. Most plastics can be traced right back to our friend petroleum. Here's how it works, in three easy steps:

1. Petroleum is found and drilled. Wells spout; men dance arm in arm; homes in Beverly Hills are purchased.

2. Petroleum is split into a number of different chemicals and gases, two of which are ethane and propane.

3. Almost magically, ethane and propane are transformed into ethylene and propylene, which are further transformed into cups and tablecloths and shoes and dental equipment and condoms and bedspreads and bracelets and clipboards and pens, into the many objects we hold so dear and take for granted, the objects upon which our dreams are hung.

*

Norman Mailer, Pulitzer Prize-winning author and activist, and famous hater of plastic (and by extension enemy of a marketplace and society so very dominated by one fossil fuel out of which we are running quickly), railing against the "triumph of the mediocre," of which the existence of plastic was a brightly glowing neon sign, said this:

> Children grow up sucking on this stuff. There's nothing, your fingertips feel nothing. If you touch a glass, you feel a little, but you touch wood you feel quite a bit, but when you touch this, nothing comes back...

And furthermore!

Nobody's ever been nourished by plastic: it's functional. It's the spiritual equivalent of political correctness: it's functional. It serves a purpose, and the cost of serving this purpose is enormous…

I imagine that Mailer had a good deal of trouble living in Our World Today. For example, the keyboard on which I am currently typing is plastic. My computer's mouse is plastic. My glasses' frame is plastic; the big headphones that hang on a hook above my desk are plastic; the speakers flanking my computer are plastic; the Philadelphia Phillies hat that sits on the shelf above me is also, distressingly, a plastic, as it is proudly made in the USA from 100 percent polyester.

*

When I was an undersized, puberty-ravaged preteen, for several years running I had a recurring dream that I was a cybernetically enhanced SuperCop, with one eye from which I could shoot piercing laser beams, and a super-strong steel hand. I had this dream so many times, and enjoyed having it so much, that I began to try to will myself to have it when in bed at night. I'd lie there, thinking of how awesome it'd be to be a laser-beam-eye- and crushing-steel-fist-having Cyborg Super Cop: *what's that in your hand? A gun? ZAP! I've just melted it with my laser beam eye, and now have you helpless in a crushing steel grip.* Everyone would think I was cool, and most importantly girls would finally note my existence.

My love affair with all things cyborg—the definition of which word is "a life form with both biological and artificial components"— persisted for years. I recall watching the series of *Star Trek: the Next Generation* episodes involving the Borg (an evil, futuristic race of cyborgs) with an almost religious pleasure. I've seen the 1987 movie *Robocop* far too many times to count. I taught myself how to draw an anime-style self-portrait by studying the video game character Mega

Man (an android superhero, with a large blue cannon for a left hand), starting with his often-surprised face (he had a lot of enemies) and laying my own glasses and dark hair over the template of his features. It was almost as if I, an ignorant and dorky kid, was unconsciously aware of the fact that people were from time to time plugged into, but, moreover, was excited about the prospect of being so connected. After all, wasn't I surrounded by machines and plastic all of the time? Wasn't technology a good thing, a force of good, a force leading to laser-beam-eyes and swift justice? Were I a cyborg, being hooked up to machines would be No Big Deal, and I would look forward to my medical future with the sort of mute anticipation one feels for those things one has been through a million times before. What, you want to put a port into my chest just above my clavicle? Knock yourself out, bro. Just make sure you don't scratch my adamantium breastplate in the process, okay?

So, standing there in the cancer clinic's chemo corridor, leaning against a wall awkwardly, watching my mother passively receive her medicine through the hole in her chest, I couldn't help but be struck by all of the plastic that surrounded my mother's frail body, which moved in and out of her as if its doing so was natural. After all, we begin our days connected to our mothers at the stomach. I was stupefied by the way the needle slipped with such little effort into my mother's port, and how, with its tubing leading from her body to the blinking box regulating her medicine, it looked for all the world like she was being *plugged* into and was being *charged*. In a way, this was, and still is, the strangest aspect of my mother's cancer to me. Once my mother had her port inserted into her chest, she became more than just my mother: she became Mommy 2.0. Once she and the port were introduced to each other (Frannie, Port. Port, Frannie) she *literally* became a cyborg, at least according to the strictest definition of the word. She became a new and improved version of my mother who could easily, repeatedly receive medicines into her bloodstream without even once being stabbed incorrectly by some tired nurse searching for a vein. She became part of a system, a mule, a vessel, an experiment, a pathway. And it strikes me that it was this body that my mother took to the grave and not the unadulterated one she called home her entire life, before the cancer, and its treatment.

*

How to draw one's self as a Surprised Anime-Android:

- **Begin with the right eye** (your left, his right): draw a quick horizontal line, and then starting from that line draw a half-circle above it. Draw two more half-circles inside the original, and color the innermost one in fully.
- **Draw the nose**: make a check mark down and to the right of the right eye.
- **Draw the left eye**: as above, for the right eye.
- **Draw the mouth**: starting somewhat below and to the right of the nose, draw an oval that ends in a point, the point being below and to the right of the nose. Fill in the mouth with a tongue (two curved bumps at the bottom of the mouth) and teeth (a line curving across the mouth's top).
- **Now draw the rest of the face**, simply by encasing all you've drawn in an oval (narrowing slightly at the chin), and adding little half-moon ears to either side of the head (that line up with the middle of the eyes).
- **Add a shock of hair** that hangs down over the forehead towards the left eye, and two eyebrows pointed up, in an expression of surprise because, per above, androids are often surprised.

What I can't tell at this point is whether the expression on the android's face is surprise or fear. It's hard to say; as many times as I've drawn a self-portrait as an anime character, my face's expression ends up looking less like surprise than it does sudden horror. Obviously the eyebrows are the problem, but complicating matters is the fact that his mouth is agape in what seems to be a silent shout. It is as if my self-portrait is aware of things that I am not yet, as if he has seen something that is only visible to drawings like him, as if he is trying to warn me about something.

Or it's as if my self-portrait doesn't particularly like being drawn as a cartoon android—please Kevin, please, Kevin, Kevin, just draw me as you are, don't make me look like I'm a cybernetic SuperCop, Kevin, Kevin, Kevin—because maybe because being an android or cyborg isn't all it's cracked up to be—no, please don't plug into me again, god no, not that, please, no, please, no, no—because maybe, just maybe, androids don't like having tubes inserted into their bodies any more than our cancer-ridden loved ones do, because of what being plugged into has come to mean: that you are not well, nor are you likely to be as you once were, not ever, never again.

IV

Leave Death to the Professionals

"IT'S NOT THE DEAD, YOU KNOW, THAT CAN HURT YOU. IT'S THE LIVING."

It is hardly worth mentioning how the Internet contains multitudes. If one is interested in something, it is likely on the Web. But knowing a fact does not diminish the power of that fact; that I, when doing research for an essay, can more or less instantly find far more information than I need about the embalming of human bodies, still amazes me.

But broad information is easy. It's really the gems that one turns up during searches on things like embalming that are what makes those searches truly worthwhile. For example, Chicago's Benson Family Funeral Home—"providing professional, compassionate care for over 40 years"—has its own YouTube channel, to which the Benson Family Funeral Home has added a number of funeral-home-related videos, including one on embalming. Almost certainly appropriated from another production—the picture's margins are cut off, and its action has clearly been incised from a longer piece, which looks to have been filmed in the heyday of VHS—the video features a delightful Hawaii-based, tattooed embalmer named Yolanda Milligan. Milligan, whose manner is more reminiscent of a bartender than someone who works with dead bodies all day, walks her viewers through the embalming process in an extremely matter-of-fact way. That the thing she is handling in the video is a dead human body, a former living person who not long before ending up on Yolanda's slab was taking labored breaths and staring unblinkingly into space as their end approached, is hardly apparent from Milligan's attitude.

Which is blithe. Milligan has the serious-yet-breezy air of a tour guide describing a place—say a stop on the Underground Railroad—that in its day must have been fraught with terror and danger but is now relegated to the minor role of an afternoon's entertainment.

To wit: as Milligan—who is garbed in full protective medical regalia, with a blue gown and tall rubber boots and thick rubber gloves and an ominous splatter-resistant face shield—stands over a dead body whose fluids she is currently exchanging with embalming fluid, she intones cheerfully that people "are afraid of death, so any care of the dead is frightening to them. I try to demystify it for them, because too many people are death-phobic. And they shouldn't be, there's no reason to be. It's not the dead, you know, that can hurt you. It's the living."

And of course she's right, but again, just because one knows something does not necessarily mean that one's knowledge of that something determines their reaction to that something. Said more simply, yes, I know the dead can't hurt me, but they still freak me out. The dead have features that are waxy and well, lifeless, oddly composed in a way that does not indicate rest but absence and the void. The first time I saw a dead body up close I knew, even as a kid, that what I was seeing was diametrically opposed to life and living, and I wanted nothing more than to get out of that church and away from all the serious adults, even if said dead body was my father's father. At any rate, it was too sunny to be indoors.

INFORMATION ACCRUAL AS PARANOIA REINFORCEMENT

Following is a partial list of diseases and conditions I have, in my role as a healthcare writer and editor, written about over the last few years, and a brief description of each, where appropriate:

- **Opioid dependence in infants**
- **Concussions and traumatic brain injuries**
- **Myelomeningocele**: more commonly called spina bifida, this is a developmental disorder in which a fetus's spinal column develops improperly
- **Muscular Dystrophy**

- **Cornelia deLange Syndrome**: a genetic disease associated with deformed limbs, growth issues, heart defects, and mental retardation
- **Fertility issues following prepubescent cancer treatments**
- **Beckwith-Wiedemann Syndrome**: a genetic overgrowth syndrome that can present as macroglossia—an enlarged tongue—and/or hemihypertrophy, when one side of the body is bigger than the other
- **Medulloblastoma**: the most common type of malignant brain tumor seen in children
- **Epilepsy**
- **Fibrodysplasia Ossificans Progressiva**: in which soft tissue like muscles ossify, resulting in restricted movement, eventual paralysis, and, often, early death

"IN ITALY FOR THIRTY YEARS UNDER THE BORGIAS THEY HAD WARFARE, TERROR, MURDER AND BLOODSHED BUT THEY PRODUCED MICHELANGELO, LEONARDO DA VINCI, AND THE RENAISSANCE. IN SWITZERLAND THEY HAD BROTHERLY LOVE, THEY HAD 500 YEARS OF DEMOCRACY AND PEACE AND WHAT DID THAT PRODUCE? THE CUCKOO CLOCK!"

The 1949 film *The Third Man* might be my favorite movie. Written by Graham Greene, the movie is a film noir masterpiece with what has got to be the best and possibly only zither-based score in cinematic history. Nearly everything about *The Third Man* is perfect: its cinematography is excellent, as the movie is just packed with stunningly composed shots of postwar Vienna; the plot, though perhaps a bit treadworn at times (a stranger comes to town; there's a mysterious woman; there are betrayals and tragedies) is extremely entertaining; Orson Welles is in it, at the height of his powers; the aforementioned zither-based score crackles; and the film is often surreal, with a handful of abstract, artistic and bizarre scenes to make one wonder how the filmmakers got away with making it in the late 1940s. It's also about a writer going on an adventure, which holds a special sort of appeal for obvious reasons.

And then there's the dialog, which is as snappy and witty and intelligent as in any film of *The Third Man*'s era, or movie history in general. Two exchanges in particular stand out: the section title above is uttered by Welles during an extremely tense scene on a Ferris wheel during which the audience wonders if Welles, the movie's villain, who is guilty of selling counterfeit penicillin that has caused the deaths of children, among others, will perhaps kill his old friend Joseph Cotten's character Holly Martins, who is the protagonist and plays a down-at-the-heels writer who initially comes to Vienna to take some sort of nebulous and ill-defined job with Welles, whom Cotten does not know is a criminal when he takes the job. Welles apparently ad-libbed the above lines and, delivered as they are high above war-ravaged Vienna on a Ferris wheel of all things, they are poignant, to say the least.

However, my favorite exchange has to be the following, between Martins and Trevor Howard's Major Calloway:

> **Calloway:** I'm not interested in whether a racketeer like Lime was killed by his friends or by an accident. The only important thing is that he's dead … I'm sorry.
>
> **Martins:** Tactful too, aren't we Callahan?
>
> **Calloway:** Calloway. Go home Martins, like a sensible chap. You don't know what you're mixing in, get the next plane.
>
> **Martins:** As soon as I get to the bottom of this, I'll get the next plane.
>
> **Calloway:** Death's at the bottom of everything, Martins.

Leave death to the professionals.

Martins: Mind if I use that line in my next Western?

What cannot be indicated by this transcription is just how quick the above exchange is. From the beginning of Calloway's first line to the lilt in Martins's voice at the end of "Western," the whole thing lasts about twenty-five seconds, and in fact speeds up toward its end; the last two lines are delivered so quickly that they almost overlap. One can imagine Cotten watching Howard's lips so that he could immediately jump in with "Mind if I…" once Howard lisped out the –s at the end of "professionals." It is this speed, in part, that is what attracts me to this particular exchange. Something significant happens almost before the viewer is aware that something has happened. And the rejoinders and wonderful writing don't hurt this back-and-forth's cause. That "leave death to the professionals" is followed immediately by "mind if I use that line in my next Western" undermines Calloway's quip with one that is more cutting and more interesting in that it breaks the fourth wall a bit. This exchange is like listening to two men who hate each other whisper "fuck you" back and forth across a crowded restaurant without any of the other patrons being aware of the hissing recriminations, subsumed as they are by the white noise of stemware being set down and cutlery engaged in its business below controlled conversations about the limits of one's career and basement renovation projects without end.

Death in the Family

My family's business was, for a time, death. More specifically, my grandfather, and his father before him, ran a funeral home, in which my father and his brothers lived while they were children, at least for a time.

Though I had no personal experience of my father's childhood funeral home home—my grandfather sold the business before I came along—when I learned that my father had for a time lived in a funeral home—upstairs, above the first floor showing room and reception areas and office, etc.—I understood to a much greater extent why my grandfather seemed so menacing in his silences and chain smoking (he was the sort of man who would keep baseballs hit by other children into his yard) but mainly thought it was deeply creepy that my dad and his brothers had grown up in a funeral home.

Not that I can attribute any odd behavior to the funeral home childhood; neither my father nor my uncles were, for example, bizarrely obsessed with the dead. All turned out to be good citizens and generally upstanding members of society. Several are well off. Rather, what does make sense is the sense of formality and rightness of behavior that so pervades my paternal side, a sense of how one should carry oneself manifested as a sort of rigidity, perhaps attributable to growing up above a showroom for the dead. For funeral homes are temples to right behavior. Some family history: When there was a viewing going on in the living room, my grandmother would hustle my father and his brothers upstairs far from the mourners, where the boys couldn't be heard, into the bathroom to play quietly with toy boats in the bathtub.

After all, when in a funeral home, one is supposed to exhibit control and tact, speaking in hushed tones when speaking at all. People visit funeral homes at vulnerable times in their lives, when they want to be treated as gently as possible, and this desire to be coddled extends to funeral homes, where the recently deceased are expected to be treated as gently as, if not more gently than, the deceased's survivors. At no time are the dead more respected and recalled positively than immediately following their demise, when their demise is still unreal, and so the deceased's survivors—who may in fact still be weeping—want to feel as if the deceased is being treated specially.

Imagine running a business catering wholly to such a sensitive clientele. And then imagine growing up above and surrounded by such a business of muted tones and patted hands, of reassuring Bible verses and stacks of laminated funeral cards and mints by the front door, next to the garlands. One imagines a childhood largely devoid of exuberance, toy boats in a hushed bathroom, the only sound that of sloshing water.

SMOTHER, SMOTHERS, SMOTHERING

One of the great truisms of life is that the more one learns about something, the more one learns how layered and recondite that something is, and how that seemingly simple something is in fact the product of hard work and human ingenuity and organization so ponderous that that something's existence seems superhuman. Supply chains are one example of this. When I worked in book publishing, when I learned of the labyrinthine route the books I helped sell—books which themselves are unbelievably complicated to even put together as a manuscript, starting in a writer's head and on a blinking white screen and the endless organization of chapters and cutting and eliding and revising and adding new material all while trying to keep the book's original idea and architecture in one's head, and then the manuscript going out into the world and ending up in an agent's hands, an agent who crafts her own sales pitch and proposal and who often does much of the heavy lifting of writing and editing that proposal themselves, all so that said proposal can hold an editor's attention long enough to impress them enough to want to take a chance on the full manuscript, which will have to be copy edited and laid out and packaged and marketed before going out into the world—take in order to get from publisher's warehouses to distribution centers, which are just bigger warehouses, to bookstores to customers' bags to customers' dusty bookshelves, I was amazed. Warehouses, which look from the road like big rectangular buildings in which workers' souls are slowly squished, are as finely tuned as handmade watches, with shipments moving in and then sorted and then out in a ballet of buzzing capitalist efficiency.

And, obviously, medicine as well. The years I spent as a science writer (a field into which I fell nearly unawares, writing about subjects I understood just enough to scare me) showed me that the daily work of understanding and treating, not to mention curing, disease is abstruse beyond belief. It is also a world surrounded by and limned on all sides by human frailty and mortality: all of the work done is in service to and because of death and death's outriders, disease, decrepitude, and suffering. All medical studies or projects, even in their most basic stages, even for the most minor conditions, exist because something has gone wrong, and doctors are seeking to right or at least understand that wrong. Though death is rarely spoken of, its specter hangs over the medical world like none other I know. My guess is one would have to make a career switch to the exciting universe of the soldier of fortune, or death row prison guard, to experience something similar.

This constant concern, this fact that every conversation is part of a larger raging against the dying of the light, to paraphrase Dylan Thomas, is exhausting. I wish, for example, that my friend Frank had not told me years ago that most of the food at whichever one of those ubiquitous casual-dining restaurant chains where he'd worked in high school was frozen and microwaved as customers ordered it. Why would I want to eat out at a restaurant where everything was microwaved? And I wish, often, that so much of my work was not inspired by and about disease, for thinking about disease day in and day out at the expense of say, the weird nightmarish histrionics going on in Bosch's *The Garden of Earthly Delights,* or the very existence and popularity of Frank Zappa's career, can make one forget that parts of the world aside from those that herald its end exist.

"THE HUMAN BODY BECOMES A CANVAS, FOR MY PARTICULAR ART."

But back to Yolanda and the aptly named "The Embalming Process. mp4." The video, true to Yolanda's promise, does indeed demystify embalming. Over music that is jauntier than one would expect—it has an island feel—Milligan explains how embalming offers "that act of closure" to grieving families because it allows them to see the deceased "in the casket, touch them…it's really important for them."

So what is the embalming process? After the body is washed, the limbs are massaged to chase away their rigor mortis and the face is "fixed," i.e., made up, the mouth is closed (sometimes with needle and thread), and caps are placed over the eyes to keep them closed and hide any sinking in the sockets. Then the body's fluids are exchanged for embalming fluid. Yolanda's fluid, in the video in question, "has a lanolin base, gives a nice texture and coloration to the tissue." Afterward the deceased is groomed and dressed. "One of the skills of embalming is to find the fine line between embalming for preservation and embalming for appearance," she intones knowingly. And unsurprisingly, an embalmer's work is often solitary. Milligan's days at work are largely spent alone, save for the company of the dead. "Nobody comes back here," she says. "Nobody ever bothers me. I'm all by myself. It's just me … and my buddies, my guests, as I like to call them. And here we go," she exclaims, as she inserts a hose into a port she's opened in a corpse's right common carotid artery, "we're off!"

After saying, "it is a body, but you know the spirit is gone. It's just an empty shell," Milligan notes how she believes in spirits but has never communed with one or seen one, much to her disappointment. However, her coworker Bonnie "can see spirits, she can feel them, she can communicate with them somehow," Yolanda says. "I'm kind in envy of her in a way." And then the video ends abruptly.

As humanizing as the video is—with its music, and interviews with Milligan's bemused boss (who saw an embalming once and that was enough, thank you very much) and the aforementioned receptionist-mystic—it is this moment at the end, a shot of Milligan's face, slack with disappointment, as she stands in front of a row of sheet-covered corpses, that defines the video. Perhaps Milligan can't communicate with her guests because she is a professional, because perhaps being a professional means that one must maintain a certain distance from the things one works with. Or perhaps being a professional means one must surround oneself with the things one works with to such an extent that one forgets about, or at least cannot pay enough attention to, other things in the world. Which in the case of those who surround themselves with death is life.

Perhaps this isn't exactly fair; after all, not everyone takes their work home with them. Maybe I—with my head filled with the details of diseases I barely understand but nonetheless fear I or my wife or, worst of all, my son might someday develop, if we haven't already—am the one who is the aberration. But nonetheless there's something in the look on Milligan's face that makes me wonder. Watched at one-quarter speed, Milligan's expression at the end of the video seems especially dramatic. Her eyes are downcast and mostly closed while she is talking, looking away from the camera, as if what she is revealing is painful. Milligan's mouth is turned down at the corners, and as she says "in envy of her..." a look of what appears to be distaste briefly passes over her features before she blinks and sets her mouth in a resigned facial shrug. A shrug speaking volumes about the weight the world lays on our shoulders and paths not taken and human happiness at the end of the day and how we spend what little time we have on the earth, and about those activities in which we find ourselves engaged or not engaged or working to escape, and signs and sighs of resignation. Let's leave death to the professionals.

Mostly Blackouts

THE PIZZA PARTY

Because I love pizza to distraction, when they told me that there would be pizza at the meeting, I quickly got over my aversions and agreed to check out this support group thing, or whatever it was. Arriving, I found, much to my extreme excitement, that they had not lied: there was indeed pizza, and lots of it. The pizza was pretty good, and was probably from one of those non-chain Italian American family affairs that are endemic to the Philadelphia area, as it had slightly too much cheese on top of the somewhat sweet sauce which, if you're not careful, will slide off onto the paper plate below, especially if the pizza is still very hot when you begin eating it, as it was at the meeting in question. Lunch was an amazing mess.

But what they didn't tell me was what the other kids would be like. There was the kid who could hardly pick up his pencil, his hands were shaking so. There was one of indeterminate gender drooling on him or herself, and that one whose head was so enormously swollen that he had trouble holding it up. Some wore bandages. A few twitched. Several were older than me, but many seemed younger. And in addition to their physical limitations, they all looked like unathletic dweebs. Dorky, spastic, jittery nerds.

Not that, at age twelve, I was what you would call an impressive physical specimen: I was undersized for my age, I wore glasses, and though I didn't know it at the time, puberty was sadly far in the future. I had virtually no upper-body strength; I listened to a lot of George Gershwin; my style choices were noncommittal. But I was athletic. In particular, I was nearing what I did not know then would be the apex of my career as a soccer player—the aforementioned late puberty would doom me in high school—and my position as a defending/attacking midfielder meant that I had to run around at more or less top speed, chasing the ball willy-nilly, for ninety minutes a game, not to mention during practice after school every day. While youth was obviously a factor, for several years I had pretty much endless stamina and was, as much as any twelve-year-old can be, in excellent cardiovascular shape, and looked generally hale, if a bit thin.

Which made me somewhat conspicuous at the pizza party slash epilepsy support group meeting. Not only was I able to hold my head up on my own, and eat piece after piece of pizza (to the point that I must have looked underfed), but I was also in obviously good condition. What right did I have to be at that meeting? I was nothing like the other kids there. Sure, sometimes I'd black out for a few seconds, and there was the day I woke after having had what I was later told was called a *grand mal*, but I'd never had surgery, and I certainly didn't have a tumor. I was hardly sick, if it could even be called that! As the meeting dragged on, I began to feel an awful guilt at being there, guilt coupled with revulsion, sitting in a circle on hard plastic chairs, listening to the other epileptic kids talk about their various problems and daily challenges, not wanting to have to talk about myself at all. After all, what could I say? How about you, Kevin, would you like to share something with the group? Me? Uh, I'm fine. I wish there'd been more pepperoni. I can't believe my parents forced me to come to this dumb meeting. It's ridiculous! I'm nothing like you stupid nerds and spazzes, nothing at all. Dorks.

A Visit to the City

What set her off was that I'd forgotten to take my medication. We'd driven into the city for my appointment and I hadn't remembered to take my medication that morning so why Kevin, why did we drive all the way into the city Kevin my mother wanted to know, as she drove in circles around the crowded, darkened underground parking lot. Cursing on her part and cringing on mine.

Driving into the city was neither an easy nor regular thing for my mother. On the rare occasions that my family came into Center City, either my father drove, or we took the train. And driving was never something my mother was very comfortable with, even under the best of circumstances. Before my father's death she hardly drove at all, and even after he died, when she was behind the wheel constantly, her driving was tentative and skittish. She was the kind of driver who would check her blind spots over and over before changing lanes, and then go so slowly that other drivers would swerve wildly around her.

Therefore the morning in question (years before my father's death) driving me into Center City for my appointment at The Children's Hospital of Philadelphia (known locally as CHOP, an unfortunate nickname for a hospital) was stressful, even before my confession about having forgotten to take my medicine. To get into Center City from our house, one took Chestnut all the way. Though offering a straight shot from the suburbs to where CHOP is located, Chestnut runs one-way, and presents suburban drivers who aren't comfortable with city traffic with a number of challenges. The lights along Chestnut are timed: if one is lucky and does approximately thirty miles per hour the entire way, one will not get stuck at a light. However, one is not always lucky, which can make for much crazy speeding up and/or slowing down to catch and/or stop suddenly at lights. Chestnut, despite being many lanes wide, also passes directly through a highly residential neighborhood, and so there is the attendant double parking, turning out of the middle lane, the clanging encroachments of emergency vehicles, and so on, which can be overwhelming. Add to that the fact that much of the neighborhood Chestnut runs through is seriously poor, especially so at the time of the drive in question. And then, when you do finally emerge from West Philly into University City, you're in University City, and must drive through a college campus crowded with undergraduates ignoring lights, and distracted pedestrians, and taxis, and then the area around the hospital itself, with its myriad ambulances and lunch carts and cops directing traffic and feeble people in wheelchairs being unloaded from idling buses, and then the narrow, claustrophobic entrance to CHOP's poorly lit underground garage that must be circled over and over again until you find a spot that is just too small to pull in easily, and so you must perform a ten-point turn to wedge your car into the space, running late for your appointment (which is concerned with human frailty, no small source of anxiety) all the while.

The Longest Night

First we watched the 1990 action-comedy Arnold Schwarzenegger vehicle *Kindergarten Cop,* in which Schwarzenegger plays a hard-charging, infrequently shaven cop who goes undercover as a tender-hearted kindergarten teacher (to obvious comedic effect) to catch a drug kingpin. After *Kindergarten Cop*, it was time for 1975's *The Man Who Would Be King*, which I now realize was for my father, as *The Man Who Would Be King* is not, despite its PG rating, the most appropriate movie for a twelve-year-old boy to watch, particularly an excitable twelve-year-old who needs to stay up all night so that he can undergo a sleep-deprived EEG.

A "test to measure the electrical activity of the brain," according to the National Institute of Health's MedlinePlus ("Trusted Health Information for You") service, an electroencephalogram (EEG) involves placing "flat metal discs" on a patient's scalp in order to monitor brain activity: "The disks are held in place with a sticky paste. The electrodes are connected by wires to a recording machine. The machine changes the electrical signals into patterns that can be seen on a monitor or drawn on paper. It looks like wavy lines."

And a sleep-deprived EEG is just what it sounds like: an EEG performed when a patient has been deprived of sleep (to better measure unusual brain activity). In my case, I had to stay up all night. Or rather, my parents had to make sure I stayed up all night. To wit, from CHOP's current sleep-deprived EEG instructions: "Make sure the child has had a good breakfast to maintain energy level. We also advise that parents take turns staying up with the child and keep him/her active if physically permissible (i.e., jumping jacks, jump rope) to stay awake."

Suffice it to say jumping jacks or any other form of jumping didn't occur during the night in question. I also wasn't being tested at CHOP, despite my doctor being based there—the testing had been relegated to some other hospital, the name of which I can no longer remember but do know it was near a Roy Rogers, as the next morning after my test was done I got to have fried chicken and biscuits at some absurdly early time in the morning. Nonetheless, the paucity of jumping-related stay-awake activities in no way undermined what I thought was going to be a great night of exciting fun in our poorly insulated TV room/porch. I, unlike my parents, found the idea of staying up all night to be exciting; at twelve I didn't consider the next-day implications of not getting enough sleep. Rather, the night before my EEG was a chance to hang out and watch fun awesome movies and have snacks, yeah!

By the time my parents changed shifts and my father took over, at some point well after midnight, I was hardly able to stay awake. Which is when, roughly, my father and I began *The Man Who Would Be King*. Starring Michael Caine and Sean Connery, the film is based on the Kipling story of the same name, and is about two adventurous ex-army rogues who travel to what is now Afghanistan and convince the locals that one of them, Connery, is a god, in a bid to rip said locals off. But of course Connery's character is not a god, so things end badly: one of the last scenes of the film is of Connery being forced to walk out on a rope bridge that the angry locals then cut, resulting in his death. But while waiting on the bridge, wearing a crown he had fashioned back when his godhead wasn't in question, Connery begins singing:

A glorious band, the chosen few on whom the Spirit came,
Twelve valiant saints, their hope they knew, and mocked
     the cross and flame.
He met the tyrant's brandished steel, the lion's gory mane,
He bowed his head his death to feel...

Then the bridge is cut and he falls and Caine, who has also been captured, looks stricken. I was in a half-awake, half-dreaming state for much of the movie, barely able to make sense of Caine's and Connery's thick Cockney and Scottish accents, respectively, much less the film's meandering adult themes. But the dread: that I remember. At some point the mood of my fun night of sleep deprivation and snacks had gone from a night colored by a thoughtless Schwarzenegger action-comedy ("It's not a tumor!") to one of fear, thanks to a film about hubris and the intimate proximity we all share with the void, ruin and poor decisions and the dread thereof. The porch had grown chilly.

A Lap to Lie In

Mostly, I blacked out.

Which is to say: Most of my seizures were almost imperceptible, or so I was told; I would slip into unconsciousness for a few seconds, seeming to others around me as if I had simply spaced out or stopped paying attention, after which I would pop back into the world, having missed the last few seconds of whatever the teacher was saying. Had my epilepsy been restricted to those sorts of seizures alone, it might have gone untreated and undetected. However, the one *grand mal* I had while on my feet—the other occurred during the aforementioned sleep-deprived EEG—was what eventually sent me to CHOP.

What happened, as I both remember and was later told, is that in the fall of sixth grade I was reading a passage from the New Testament aloud in the cold gymnasium of my new school where we were practicing for Confirmation, and while reading I collapsed and went unconscious and began to have one those classically upsetting seizures, with the shaking limbs and the eyes having rolled up into my head and I guess there was also worry that I might bite off my tongue while shaking and trembling. What I do remember is standing at the podium one moment, nervously looking out at the crowd of my classmates, aware of how new I was and how I didn't really know anyone and especially aware of the redheaded girl, and then suddenly waking up in the soft ponderous lap of the school's terrifying principal. And then the wave of shame and embarrassment that followed as soon as I was awake enough to see the looks of horror and shock and even in a few cases gleeful malice on the faces of my new classmates, whom I so had wanted to befriend.

But mostly, I just blacked out, which no one seemed to notice much.

THOSE AWFUL CHILLS

Sold under a number of different brand names, including Depakote, valproic acid is an anticonvulsant that per MedlinePlus "is used alone or with other medications to treat certain types of seizures." Valproic acid is associated with a number of side effects, some of them serious. These include dizziness, drowsiness, mood swings and weight changes, diarrhea and hair loss. More serious are valproic acid's association with serious liver damage, and the ways in which serious liver damage presents: nausea, vomiting, yellowing of the eyes or skin, and facial swelling. My particular cross to bear was diarrhea. Lots and lots of diarrhea.

When you're driving in a Chevy and you feel something heavy /
Diarrhea! / Diarrhea!

When I was first prescribed Depakote, I couldn't swallow pills. At first my mother would break my pills in half—they were filled with tiny granules—and pour the pills' innards into bowls of applesauce. This tasted awful. Eventually I graduated to swallowing smaller amounts of applesauce in which the unbroken pills were encased. And from there moving to pills-and-water and then pills-and-almost-no-water was a relatively easy transition. But the first few months I was on Depakote were marked by much choking and gagging and whining.

When you're climbing up a ladder and you feel something splatter /
Diarrhea! / Diarrhea!

In 2012, the United States Department of Justice announced that the manufacturer of Depakote, Abbott Laboratories, had "pleaded guilty and agreed to pay $1.5 billion to resolve its criminal and civil liability arising from the company's unlawful promotion of the prescription drug Depakote for uses not approved as safe and effective." Abbott was illegally promoting Depakote for unapproved uses, namely to treat elderly patients with dementia. This is in addition to the fact that valproic acid is generally not recommended for children under the age of ten—I was a small-for-my-age twelve when I began taking it—and tthat valproic acid/Depakote is associated with "hepatic failure resulting in fatalities has occurred in patients receiving valproate and its derivatives," according to the big nasty black box found on the third page of Depakote's official prescribing information. In addition, certain cross-Atlantic agencies—the UK, the EU—suggest that valproic acid/valproate/Depakote and its ilk not be prescribed to children under eighteen for mood disorders.

When you're sliding into first and you feel something burst / Diar-
rhea! / Diarrhea!

I could hardly eat. I was so thin and so pale all of the time, and my hair seemed to have rather bizarrely begun to become wavy where before it was straight. Much of what I did eat came out of me in hosing gushes of ass piss, several times a day; for several years running I didn't really take a solid shit. I went to the bathroom so often that I almost grew used to the way my body handled nausea; I grew accustomed to diarrhea's sine wave of relief and distress. What I never could get used to, however, was having to constantly ask to go to the bathroom. I could tell that I annoyed some of my less sympathetic teachers, and every time I put my hand up to ask I was telling my classmates (to all of whom I still something of a stranger) that there was something wrong with me. Ah yes, the sick kid, they no doubt thought every time I excused myself, sometimes for the third or fourth time in a class period. I knew, with a firm certainty, how and almost exactly when anything I ate would exit my body. An hour, maybe two, later, and my hand would be up again, or I'd be sequestered in a bathroom in my house with a book, waiting for the next break between bouts of diarrhea to begin, surrounded by my own stench so often that it began to fill my nostrils, permanently pushing out the world's other smells in lieu of its heat and sharp insistent sourness. I can smell it still.

A Brighter Shade of

The house was pink so that's how it got the name "The Pink House," though the house's color was less of a proper pink than a lighter shade thereof, more of faded, dirtied cotton candy, but "The Cotton Candy House" sounds less like the name of a house than that of a business whose customer base consists of children hopelessly addicted to sugary treats, so "The Cotton Candy House" might not have been so inappropriate a name after all, as "The Pink House" functioned much of the time less as a house than as a repository and enabler of juvenile behavior, specifically alcohol-related juvenilia:

e.g., continuous punch parties; and those involving vodka encased in Jello; and pre-Thanksgiving dinners attended by people in their late teens and early twenties playing grownup, wherein the attendants couldn't tell if their drowsiness was from the turkey or the boxes of red wine, or the bongs; and far more frequently those parties thrown for no discernible reason, and with no theme aside from the rapid consumption of beer, at one of which events, standing on the back porch of the colored house in question, I once got a can of economy beer caught on my lower lip as I was attempting to shotgun it—

shotgunning being a manner of drinking a canned beverage wherein one tears a hole in the side of the can with some implement, such as one's keys and, after opening the beverage's top one tilts one's head sideways and rapidly pours (for to call what one does when one shotguns *drinking* would be to demean the act of drinking) whatever it is that is in the can, in this case beer, rapidly down one's throat via the new hole, the pouring process sped up by the extra air flow the hole provides

—and it was much to the delight of several of those in attendance that I got said can caught on my lip but not to my own delight, as I had a can caught on (read: *in*) my lower lip, the hole I'd created in the can's side being jagged and pointy, having used to make the hole the dull key to my mother's house several hundred miles to the east, in which she was blissfully unaware of what I was doing with the key to her back door, and I am sure that I thought about how my mother would disapprove of my behavior in the strongest possible terms, and of me generally, half-drunk on a sagging porch in rural Ohio trying to wrest a can of beer from my bloody lip while one of my fellow partygoers literally pointed and laughed at me, as if seeing an undergraduate drunkenly injure himself is the funniest thing in the world, a guy

who was older than all of us, he had facial hair and long, dark hair, I think he was an alumnus and was therefore someone who at the time I thought should have been mature enough to realize that there is a time and place for drinking cheap beer with college students in small towns in Ohio and that one should not in general participate in such activities as an "adult" (and should not, moreover, mercilessly heckle those who hurt themselves in so doing), which I now am, an adult: I pay bills; I get into bed around 10 PM; I am a commuter and a parent; I understand the importance of life insurance; I proactively take allergy medication;

and I remember such moments from my youth in the same way I imagine my mother would have thought of them then had she been so aware, with a palpable sense of disgust, and it strikes me now, years later, how few of my memories I can recall with pride or happiness, and how much of what I remember well are those things I'd in fact rather forget, but in lieu of being able to recall very much about my father, for instance, who died while I was in college, my mind is instead filled with bullshit like the details of a pink, run-down, three-bedroom house in which I did not live, and in which I constantly drank myself insensible for several years running: the fake-oak-paneled dining room where we played beer pong; the way the living room's filthy, off-white couch sagged in the center and pushed at its seams; and most of all the kitchen, the eastern wall of which had a walk-in pantry where the punch would go, when there were punch parties, which was often.

The list of things I'd prefer to forget goes on and on, for in the years following college I continued to embarrass myself on a pretty regular basis, proving that I am not one of those people who instantly embrace adulthood—the sorts who upon getting their first job in the real world by the age of twenty-three have married, begun the process of procreating, and taken on a mortgage—but am instead one of those people who wander slowly into adulthood's neighborhood and decide after more wandering, lost within the boundaries of adulthood's neighborhood, to check out the new restaurant that just opened up down the street, to mix metaphors

as cruelly as I have tested my Irish-Catholic ability to feel deep and constant shame. Which, as clichéd as the Irish shame thing might be, is something I nonetheless admit to being a victim of, as I am nearly always ashamed of my life and past and the person I used to be, either because of embarrassing things I have done, such as getting a can of beer caught on my lower lip while binge drinking, or simply being ashamed of those now-unfashionable clothes I used to wear, or the unfortunate period, again during college, when I thought it was funny while out at night to drunkenly yell DUDE! WHAT? DUDE!! WHAT?? at the top of my lungs, in sad imitation of the forgettable stoner movie *Dude, Where's My Car?*; i.e., shame at having acted, in the past, like a douchebag, which recognition leads to anxiety about whether any of my present actions will lead to any future shame re: acting like a douche, such as going on *ad nauseum* about this one dumb time I got a can caught on my lip like it was an event in my life that meant something when really, it wasn't, at least not compared to the big events in our lives, the ones that are the architects of our dreams, like the death of one's father when one is eighteen, but no, that's not fair either, because were all such small moments, even those shameful ones, truly forgettable, what would be the point of remembering anything but the big things, thus making of our memories points on a sparsely populated timeline, long spaces of black nothingness punctuated by recollections of big events: BLACK birthday party BLACK waking up in the principal's fat lap after having had a seizure BLACK staying up all night with dad watching *Kindergarten Cop* BLACK: and so on, but no, color is what is wanted, some color, any.

For example. My father's mustache looms in my memories of him like an eclipse, nearly blotting out any clear recollections I might have of his appearance, unaided by photographs; when I think of my father's face, I mainly see his mustache. I have trouble remembering what color his eyes were—I think they might have been green—but while the rest of his features are hazy, I can quite easily recall the bristles of his mustache. For most of his adult life, my father had a serious mustache, only shaving it off a few times; when he did shave it he looked oddly undressed, and always grew it back right away. His mustache was what might be called a "full" or "natural" mustache and, as far as I know, he only ever trimmed it for length. To this day when I see well-grown mustaches on other men's faces, I feel envy and loss.

Though my father's mustache was for many years a deep, lustrous black, by the time he died it had begun to gray, and was flecked throughout with wiry gray hairs. In particular, there was one gray hair on the left side of my dad's mustache that always seemed to jut out from the main mass of hair, as if it were a mustache cowlick. Because my father was fastidiously vain about his appearance, this errant gray hair was far more noticeable than it would have been had my father not trimmed his mustache on a frequent basis. So when I looked at my father's face, I tended often as not to look at his mustache, and the way this one hair stood apart.

The hair wasn't special. It was a hair. And he never mentioned it, nor did I mention it and in so mentioning it prompt a deep father-son conversation about grooming, and the face one presents to others, how to navigate the churning waters of adulthood, and the iniquity of aging. The hair was simply there. But it is special insofar as I remember it, or at least insofar as it is a conduit for remembering something that is special; I cannot say for sure that I would much remember what my father looked like (without photographic aid) if not for that gray hair. And so that hair, which rode on my father's upper lip, a piece of anatomy I associate with watching him smile (and the way the hairs above it curled as his lip moved) and with watching him speak, helps keep my memories of my father from completely fading into the fog. Because my memory of that gray hair shines like a light in the dark, like lights on an airport runway in the deep dark of an autumn night, the lights climbing toward the end of the runway before retreating and climbing again, seemingly ascending to a point that they nearly reach but don't before attempting the ascent again. The lights signaling: land here, here is safety. Here is light and warmth, and knots of family members waiting among harried travelers and bored airport employees lounging by the luggage carousels spinning and spinning, waiting to take you home.

An Appropriate Ending

Sometimes it is less an ending than the anticipation of an ending that one wants to end, so that the ending can be got over with and, in its wake, a new beginning or some reconciliation with that ending can be made.

Anticipate: from the Latin *anticipare*, meaning "to take" and "before." When I anticipate something, I envision undergoing it. Following that, anticipation is necessarily associated with one's feelings about the thing that has not yet happened: if you fear an ending, then the anticipation you will feel about that ending will be negative, associated with a growing dread at even the merest contemplation of the ending you fear. And contrariwise regarding those endings to which you are looking forward.

*

Despite fearing many sorts of endings—of personal relationships, of a good book, of that candy bar I am eating, of life—I've always been struck by the ease with which people will approach certain sorts of endings. Take employment-related relationships. Nearly every time I have left a job, from the moment I gave notice until my ultimate departure, I noticed an emotional cooling between my coworkers and myself. Oh we may pretend over pizza or cake or alcohol that we are sad about the forthcoming departure, and maybe we really are, but the emotional cooling nonetheless occurs, as we are well aware that the end of our working together often spells an end to the ways in which our lives' edges will rub up against one another. Think of the jobs you have had and left. Then think of your former coworkers. To how many do you still speak regularly?

While one could read such coldness as a sign of selfishness—after all, when people leave jobs of their own accord it is often to go on to bigger, better things, or at the very least to get away from a place they've disliked going to so much that being paid to go there is no longer worth it—it can also be viewed less negatively: people are unable to devote much care to those things that do not directly affect them. Let's say you hear about something bad happening to someone you don't know personally, or whom you know only in passing. Providing, of course, that you aren't a sociopath, surely your sense of compassion might cause you to say something like "Oh, that's terrible," but if you are not personally acquainted with the person to whom the something bad has happened you will almost certainly return your focus to the remainder of your own day. The fact that something bad happened to someone, at some point, somewhere, will pass from your mind like a half-heard murmur.

*

Meanwhile, the deaths of pets. In 2007, I put my cat Biko to sleep. Two notes on this sentence:

1. We did not name Biko. Biko had been my wife's sister's cat: she had gotten him from a friend in Chicago, who had in turn gotten him from somewhere, and so on. Biko had been passed from owner to owner, and we were his last stop. He was named after the late South African anti-apartheid activist Steve Biko by his no doubt interesting original owner. Steve Biko was a hero, certainly, but I always thought it too obviously wry to name a black and white tabby cat after an activist who was beaten to death by thuggish racist cops.
2. I did not put Biko "to sleep." I had my veterinarian euthanize him with a very large dose of some barbiturate. Nonetheless, Biko certainly *seemed* to go to sleep. He looked at me while the vet injected him, and then he was dead, his eyes still

open. We say things like "put to sleep" to shield ourselves from the guilt associated with phrases like "I paid my vet kill my cat because my cat was dying." Such language seeks to mitigate the degree to which one is responsible for something upsetting; I did not *kill* my cat, I put him to *sleep*. That he died during his "sleep" is an unfortunate byproduct of my good intentions, and you know what they say about those.

Biko had been old and sick for some time, and was growing increasingly older and sicker every day. In addition to being seventeen or eighteen years old, Biko was terribly, unhealthily thin. Biko had for some years been suffering from hyperthyroidism, and by the time we got him was already on a daily regimen of pills-crushed-into-his-food. Though the pills treated his condition for several years, eventually death won, as it is wont to do. When it did, my wife was out of town, so it fell to me to watch this poor animal refuse to drink and eat and to shut down to the point that I had to make a trembling call to our vet, who suggested I bring him in right away.

Though I suspected when I called the vet that Biko was dying, I didn't really believe that he was actually dying right then, not yet no. But I was wrong, and our incredibly kind and soft-faced mustachioed veterinarian informed me that Biko's end was nigh and that I had best say goodbye to him then and there because this was happening right now, in just a few minutes.

Thus followed a strange, sad, episode. The vet left us alone in the examination room, so that I/we could say goodbye. Even through all the emotions and being terribly overwhelmed by everything that was going on—I was broke; my mother had been diagnosed with what turned out to be a fatal case of metastatic colorectal cancer only a few months before; and I was living in a place where I felt like a stranger—I was aware of how ridiculous saying goodbye to a dying animal who couldn't understand me even on the best of days and who certainly couldn't then, as *in extremis* as he was, and who was less a little furry person who I interacted with than a vessel for me to impart and project emotional needs onto, was. Yet there we sat, just the two of us, while I petted his bony little head and muttered *I'm going to miss you buddy,* tears welling in my eyes.

*

Much confusion rests squarely at the feet of the word *satisfaction*. Lest I wander into territory better suited for philosophers, what does the word *satisfaction* even mean? When I am satisfied after eating, I have had enough, but saying that one is satisfied with one's meal does not necessarily mean that one enjoyed one's meal. Nor, in general, does satisfaction necessarily imply happiness. It simply implies enough.

Then there is the old, for the most part forgotten, pre-duel command *I demand satisfaction,* said to the person to be dueled after that person has injured the speaker in such a manner that the speaker feels some violent confrontation is necessary. But again: the satisfaction got from a duel, assuming the challenged party agrees, does not mean the duel will turn out well for the challenger. The satisfaction then is got simply from having the duel take place, and from the catharsis attained by having the matter be solved definitively through the wounding or violent death of one or both of the duel's participants.

But a *satisfying* ending? That's a stickier wicket. We do say some endings—of movies, of good songs that do not trail off weakly, of books—are satisfying, but are they really? What does one say about a satisfying ending, after all? That it met one's expectations? That it did not disappoint? That it was tidy? Rather than defining why an ending is satisfying qua satisfying, we frequently specify other things that it was or was not. Maybe this is less of a problem of language's imprecision than the extreme malleability of the idea of endings, vis-à-vis our daily experience of things leading to things *ad infinitum.* Maybe endings, such as we might like to believe, do not really exist.

Two examples from literature:

1. Cormac McCarthy's 2005 novel *No Country for Old Men* ends neither with a bang nor a whimper, but with a dream seemingly unrelated to the action of the story at large. The novel, which is largely concerned with two men's dispute over a great deal of drug money, also features a town sheriff who follows the two men's actions. The sheriff acts as a sort of observing reader, in that he frequently stumbles upon the aftermath of the novel's main plot—because this is McCarthy, that means violence and corpses—and does a deal of sage musing thereupon. So this novel, which is ostensibly a crime novel but isn't really at all, *should* end with some sort of conclusion that neatly wraps up the plot—what happens to which character, what happens to the money, and so forth, leading to some manner of clichéd ending where someone drives off in some sort of car, listening to a Patsy Cline song on the radio—but doesn't. Instead, *No Country for Old Men* comes to a close with a deeply moving scene of the sheriff telling a story about a dream he had about his father carrying a fire bundle, and the novel ends on the sentence, "And then I woke up."

2. *Lord of the Rings* trilogy, by J.R.R. Tolkien, on the other hand, has an ending that less explodes than limps slowly to the finish, whimpering about its tired, aching limbs the whole way and, when it does come to a close, it ends on a note largely disconnected from the plot and movement and characters that defined the preceding writing. Where the trilogy's main body booms and roars and sweeps across time and space, the series's ending is a maudlin domestic set piece at odds with the bulk of the book.

a.   A short explanation: *The Lord of the Rings* trilogy is broadly about the adventures of a character named Frodo, who is a short man-like creature known as a Hobbit. In his quest to destroy an evil magic ring, Frodo is aided and opposed by various fantasy-genre stand-bys: wizards, elves, dwarves, wraiths, goblins, and so on. There are various skirmishes and battles that grow in scale until full-blown wars are being waged between the forces of good and evil. Frodo travels a great deal and misses his home. Eventually, after many hardships and brushes with death, Frodo (unwittingly aided by a rival) manages to destroy the evil magic ring by casting it into a volcano, so destroying the trilogy's antagonist.

    i.   Instead of ending on this triumphant scene—as one might expect an allegorical fantasy novel to do—Tolkien instead tracks Frodo's long journey home, and gives the readers an extended coda in which Frodo and his fellow adventurers banish the shadow of the fallen foe's evil from their homeland, which theretofore had been a land so unsullied as to be head-smackingly symbolic, its perfection and green meadows and happy chubby tiny short people chortling over their beer just crying out to be taken advantage of by some fallen evil wizard's second wizard-in-command who, minus his powers due to the ring's destruction, still possesses his influential liar's tongue and, more importantly, is at the end of his rope. Then, after Frodo and crew cleanse their land of this evil man, Frodo prepares to set sail with a group of elves for a magical land over the seas where only a select few can go and where, supposedly, no one ever dies. The book ends, finally, with Frodo's best friend Sam saying goodbye to Frodo at the dock and then returning to his home in Hobbiton, which is what the hobbits' town is named, appropriately, to kiss the wife he has gotten himself in the uncertain amount of time between getting rid of evil wizard #2 and Frodo's departure and, upon arriving home, Sam says to his wife Rosie, "Well, I'm back."

1. Which would be appropriate— as the trilogy is really a journey story—if not for the fact that it is Frodo (admittedly accompanied by Sam) who makes the journey, and, moreover, that Sam has been back for a great deal of time (back as in back in hobbit land) by the time Sam ultimately returns home to his new wife and hobbit hole (as hobbits live in magnificent holes in the sides of hills) from his short trip to the docks to say goodbye to Frodo. And, most of all, that the trilogy's ending is domestic and personal and touching while the trilogy, one could argue, is less concerned with the characters as people than it is with the characters as participants in a grand and thrilling epic quest to destroy the ring and so rid their world of evil.

Though it's probably clear by now, I find the McCarthy ending satisfying while I find the Tolkien ending unsatisfying. I admit that my reasons for approving of one but not the other are confused and subjective. After all, both the McCarthy and the Tolkien end with a bit of misdirection. Neither ending really brings its book's / trilogy's action to a complete rest, and both end on scenes that dart diagonally away from the works' timelines; I think of their direction as being *skewed,* in the sense of something bouncing at a crazy and unexpected angle, similar to when a ground ball hits the pitcher's mound and is launched in a direction so unexpected that the fielders behind the mound are unable to react quickly enough to field the ball cleanly to produce an out.

And now that I've worked baseball into the essay, the McCarthy ending is an inside-the-park home run (always unexpected; rare; happening suddenly; and accompanied by the crowd's excited cheering building to a deafening, hysterical roar) while the Tolkien ending is a weak ground ball that only gets a man on base because the second baseman was looking at a pretty lady in the seats behind home plate and, distracted, let the ball dribble through his legs and into the right field grass, where it rolled to a stop.

*

Well, what then? Would you prefer a clean break—right off, like a Band-Aid—or a trickling down of the action, a song fading slowly into silence until you are only left with the memory of the song's melody, a murmuring whisper of the experience you were having leading seamlessly into a memory of that experience? Or like a sudden light in a dark room, your eyes having no time to adjust, all of the objects that surround you momentarily thrown into near-blinding and strange illumination? Like sex, meaning the real thing, between people, where there is the reality of cleanup and bodily fluids, of handkerchiefs between legs and the urge to urinate despite not being able to pee straight, and sometimes a desire for sweets? Like a procession out of a church, behind the priest swinging his smoking censer, his robes billowing slightly as he proceeds down the aisle, past the eyes of his congregation, toward the church's double doors opened to the sunshine of the day? Like a cup of coffee you've forgotten and the bottom of which has grown cold and bitter with indifference, and that when you remember to sip from it will cause you to wrench up your mouth in a grimace of disgust?

*

The root of the adjective *appropriate,* which can be defined as "suitable" or "proper," is the Latin verb *appropriare,* "to draw near, approach." Seeking a clear, ultimate definition of a word via its etymology can be tricky, to say the least, as the search for a definition of something that is by its nature difficult to be defined via other equally malleable definitions can instead of granting clear understanding lead one directly into understanding's opposite, into further confusion and such navel-gazing relativistic muddling that rather than discovering what one was looking for one finds oneself trapped in the act of looking. Etymology can be a distracting hall of mirrors: A leads to B, which leads to C, which leads to what was I trying to figure out again?

Nonetheless, etymological inquiry can lead to some *better* understanding of what a word means. Or at least what it was intended to mean. At any rate: *appropriate.* Based on its Latin root, one could say that if something is appropriate, it draws near that to which is it appropriate; it is allowed to approach that to which it is appropriate because of its appropriate nature. But that's vague at best, and more digging is wanted, in particular into the words that define appropriate—"suitable" and "proper." The meanings of either could be *appropriate*— if something is suitable to a situation, it is appropriate thereto—which gets us nowhere; one cannot define something if that something also defines those things which it itself is defined by.

Suitable comes in part from the Old French *suitte,* "attendance," and carries with it from the 14th century a sense of attendance at court, i.e., something that is *suitable* is appropriate (there's that pesky word again!) to be worn at court, where one must look one's best if one is to stay in the King's favor. If you are dressed appropriately at court, you do not look out of place. From this it is pretty easy to see where we got our term *suit* which is what we call an uncomfortable getup one puts on before events at which it is important to be well-dressed.

Proper, on the other hand, is from the Latin *proprius,* which means one's own, or characteristic, "peculiar" (in the sense of peculiar meaning *distinctive* as opposed to *odd*). Appropriate, via this definition of proper, would then mean that whatever X is appropriate to (or vice versa) is so in a way that could be said to be personal, or has a close relationship with, or is intimate with. Again with the employment references: when deciding how to conducting oneself in a place of business, it is appropriate to be businesslike (business: Old English *bisignes, "care, anxiety"*), i.e., to modulate one's voice, to lay off the race jokes, to groom oneself regularly, to keep track of one's appointments in one's calendar, and to show one's superiors that peculiar mix of deference and defiance that lets them know they're in charge but that come annual review time one expects to be well compensated, because you're not just a cog. Which, as far as understanding what *appropriate* means, leads right back to my earlier point re: navels and gazing, and the lint to be found therein.

*

When I was eleven or twelve, my parents threw me a surprise birthday party. I have never liked being given surprise parties. In short, I do not enjoy being the center of people's attention without first being forewarned that I would be the center of people's attention. And I really was especially not into surprise parties when I was eleven or twelve or however old I was when the surprise party was thrown for me. So you can see where this is going.

In defense of my overreaction to the party in question, my father did a poor job of setting up this particular surprise. I was sitting in our family's living room reading something that may well have been one of Tolkien's *Lord of the Rings* books when my father came up to me and said,

"Kevin go ask your sisters what kind of pizza they want for dinner."

Which was a ridiculous request, because my sisters were in the room immediately next to the living room, watching television, and my father was closer to the TV room—as he was standing in the middle of the living room hallway when he made his request—than I was. Also, at that time we always got the same kind of pizzas when we ordered pizza, plain and pepperoni, so there was no need to verify my sisters' order.

"No, you ask them. I'm reading,"

I said to my father, or something along those lines. I remember having an attitude when I said this; I may have sneered. To which rejoinder my father bristled, his voice rising,

"Kevin do I what I tell you go ask your sisters what kind of pizza they want for dinner!"

And I, upping the stakes, responded firmly,

"No dad!"

And he,

"Dammit Kevin do it!"

Now things were indeed fully heated, so much so that I decided that further fighting wasn't really in my best interest.

"Fine!"

I half-shouted, aggressively putting a bookmark in my book and stomping toward the TV room, making my displeasure known. As I was walking through the doorway I asked,

"Guys what kind of pizza do you…"

when suddenly,

"SURPRISE!!!!"

and out popped a whole bunch of my friends from behind the couch, ecstatic and happy, the aforementioned surprise party, scaring the hell out of me and causing me to burst into tears. I ran upstairs to my room.

But things improved from there: my mother came and found me and, while chuckling softly to herself, made me dry my tears, and then my friends and I had what turned out to be a pretty awesome surprise birthday pizza party while playing the many Nintendo games they'd brought with them. Later, several hours later, when it was time for them to go, I was sad and did not want them to leave, such fun eating pizza and playing video games I'd been having, so much fun in fact that the experience (and therefore my memories thereof) had become for me less about the initial histrionics than about the happiness I felt while surrounded by friends and pizza and Nintendo and have I mentioned the pizza? I do love pizza.

NOTES

"The Lump in Adam's Throat"

Adam Yauch Announcement; https://youtu.be/
u7CH3M7cECI (accessed September 28, 2016).

Massimo Politi, Massimo Robiony, Claudio Avellini, and
Maria Orsaria, "Epithelial-myoepithelial Carcinoma of
the Parotid Gland: Clinicopathological Aspect, Diagnosis
and Surgical Consideration," *Annals of Maxillofacial
Surgery* 4, no. 1 (January–June 2004): 99–102.

Pubmed; https://www.ncbi.nlm.nih.gov/pubmed

"Place," in *Art in the Twenty-First Century*,
Season 1 (September 21, 2001).

"Some Kind of Wunderkammer"

The Central Intelligence Agency, The World Factbook;
https://www.cia.gov/library/publications/the-world-
factbook/ (accessed September 28, 2016).

Pope Nicholas V, "Dum Diversas." English translation
available in *Unam Sanctam Catholicam*; http://
unamsanctamcatholicam.blogspot.de/2011/02/dum-
diversas-english-translation.html (accessed September 28,
2016).

"Much Melancholy Stillness"

> J. A. Crowe, and G. B. Cavalcaselle, *Early Flemish Painters: Notices of Their Lives and Works* (London: J. Murray, 1857).

"Jason Noble's Shoulder"

> Drug Enforcement Administration, "Drug Schedules;" https://www.dea.gov/druginfo/ds.shtml (accessed September 28, 2016).

"Fuck You, Everybody"

> The quote that precedes this essay comes from a letter Clyfford Still sent to Betty Freeman on December 14, 1960. It is currently housed in the Betty Freeman Papers, Archives of American Art, Smithsonian Institution.

> The Henry T. Hopkins quote comes from Steven Henry Madoff, "Unfurling the Hidden Work of a Lifetime," *The New York Times*, March 18, 2007.

> The language from Clyfford Still's will comes from Sylvia Hochfield, "Revealing the Hidden Clifford Still," *Artnews* (January 1, 2009); http://www.artnews.com/2009/01/01/revealing-the-hidden-clyfford-still/ (accessed September 28, 2016).

"The Other Woman"

> On *The Agnew Clinic*'s commission see University of Pennsylvania, "Medical Class of 1889: Commissioning

of Thomas Eakins to Paint 'The Agnew Clinic'," in University Archives and Records Center; http://www.archives.upenn.edu/histy/features/1800s/1889med/agnewclinic.html (accessed September 28, 2016).

John Berger, *Ways of Seeing* (New York: Viking, 1973). The book is based on the 1972 BBC TV series of the same name.

David Hayes Agnew, *The Principles and Practice of Surgery: Being a Treatise on Surgical Diseases and Injuries* (Philadelphia: J. B. Lipincott 1878–83).

Sidney Kirkpatrick, *The Revenge of Thomas Eakins* (New Haven: Yale University Press, 2006).

National Center for Educational Statistics, Institute of Education Sciences, "National Assessment of Adult Literacy;" https://nces.ed.gov/naal/ (accessed September 28, 2016).

The University of Pennsylvania's Barbara Bates Center for the Study of the History of Nursing keeps an archive of Mary V. Clymer's papers. The finding aid is available on the University of Pennsylvania Libraries website; http://hdl.library.upenn.edu/1017/d/ead/upenn_bates_PUNMC16 (accessed September 28, 2016).

"That Knot in Your Stomach"

S. Kyaga, P. Lichtenstein, M. Boman, C. Hultman, N. Långström, and M. Landén, "Creativity and Mental Disorder: Family Study of 300,000 People with Severe

Mental Disorder." *British Journal of Psychiatry* 199, no. 5 (November 2011): 373–79.

Ahmed Hankir, "Review: Bipolar Disorder and Poetic Genius." *Psychiatria Danubina* 23, suppl. 1 (2011): 62–68.

Wojciech Bałus, "Dürer's 'Melencolia I': Melancholy and the Undecidable," *Artibus et Historiae* 15, no. 30 (1994): 9–21.

Read "Dream Song 29" on the Academy of American Poets website. Read it twice. Thrice: John Berryman, "Dream Song 29," in *Academy of American Poets*; https://www.poets.org/poetsorg/poem/dream-song-29 (accessed September 28, 2016).

N. Nakaya, "Effect of Psychosocial Factors on Cancer Risk and Survival," *Journal of Epidemiology* 24, no. 1 (2014): 1–6.

C. Bergelt, E. Prescott, M. Grønbæk, U. Koch, and C. Johansen, "Stressful Life Events and Cancer Risk," *British Journal of Cancer* 95 (2006): 1579–81.

Lital Keinan-Boker, Neomi Vin-Raviv, Irena Liphshitz, Shai Linn, and Micha Barchana, "Cancer Incidence in Israeli Jewish Survivors of World War II," *Journal of the National Cancer Institute* 101, no. 21 (2009): 1489–1500.

Stephen D. Hursting and Michele R. Forman, "Cancer Risk from Extreme Stressors: Lessons from European Jewish Survivors of World War II," *Journal of the National*

Cancer Institute 101, no. 21 (2009): 1436–37.

Michael R. Irwin, "Depression and Risk of Cancer
Progression: An Elusive Link," *Journal of Clinical
Oncology* 25, no. 17 (June 2007): 2343–44.

Brenda W. J. H. Penninx, Jack M. Guralnik, and Richard
J. Havlik, "Chronically Depressed Mood and Cancer
Risk in Older Persons," *Journal of the National Cancer
Institute* 90, no. 24 (1998): 1888–93.

Thomas John Papadimos, "Eluding Meaninglessness:
A Note to Self in Regard to Camus, Critical Care, and
the Absurd," *The Permanente Journal* 18, no. 1 (Winter
2014): 87–89.

"Umbrellas"

"Christo Umbrella Crushes Woman," *The New York Times*,
October 28, 1991.

M. B. Streiff, "Vena Caval Filters: A Comprehensive
Review," *Blood* 95, no. 12 (June 2000): 3669–77.

S. Amjad Hussein, "Profile: Kazi Mobin-Uddin; Surgeon-
Researcher Extraordinaire; Father of Endovascular
Surgery," *Journal of the Islamic Medical Association of
North America* 37 (2005): 78–80.

"Leave Death to the Professionals"

The Benson Family Funeral Home YouTube channel can
be found here: https://youtu.be/rc_QSyWl-GA.

United States Department of Justice, "Abbott Labs to Pay $1.5 Billion to Resolve Criminal and Civil Investigations of Off-label Promotion of Depakote," Press release from the Office of Public Affairs, May 7, 2012; https://www.justice.gov/opa/pr/abbott-labs-pay-15-billion-resolve-criminal-civil-investigations-label-promotion-depakote (accessed September 28, 2016).

OTHER NOTES & ACKNOWLEDGMENTS

Though nonfiction, and true to my experience, this book may not be entirely accurate. Memory and perspective are flawed and subjective. Some names and/or details have been modified, events manipulated, and dialogue recreated. I did my best, so any factual inaccuracies that remain are unintentional.

All etymological inquiry comes from the indispensable Online Etymology Dictionary (www.etymonline.com) or from the *Chambers Dictionary of Etymology*, edited by Robert K. Barnhart and Sol Steinmetz (Edinburgh: Chambers, 1988).

Grateful acknowledgement is made to the editors of *Pithead Chapel, Turtle Island Quarterly, The Collapsar, Tammy, Midway Journal*, and *Cobalt Review*, where several of this collection's essays first appeared.

This book is for my family.

Kevin O'Rourke lives outside Seattle, where he works as an editor and publications manager. He studied art at Kenyon College and writing at the University of Minnesota. His work has been published in *Cobalt Review, Tammy, Seneca Review,* and *The Collapsar,* among others. *As If Seen at an Angle* is his first book.